─────── MEET PAUL ───────

Donald Coggan was Archbishop of York from 1961 to 1974 and of Canterbury from 1974 to 1980. He is the author of many books, on subjects ranging from theology and biblical studies to biography and spirituality. His most recent titles include *The Servant-Son: Jesus Then and Now* (Triangle 1995) and *A New Day for Preaching* (SPCK 1996).

By the same author:

The Prayers of the New Testament (Hodder & Stoughton 1967)
Convictions (Hodder & Stoughton 1975)
On Preaching (SPCK 1978)
Sure Foundation (Hodder & Stoughton 1981)
Paul: Portrait of a Revolutionary (Hodder & Stoughton 1984)
Cuthbert Bardsley: Bishop, Evangelist, Pastor (Collins 1989)
God of Hope (Fount 1991)
The Voice from the Cross (Triangle 1993)
The Servant-Son: Jesus Then and Now (Triangle 1995)
A New Day for Preaching (SPCK 1996)

——MEET PAUL——

An Encounter with the Apostle

Donald Coggan

TRIANGLE

First published in Great Britain 1998
Triangle
Society for Promoting Christian Knowledge
Holy Trinity Church
Marylebone Road
London NW1 4DU

The publisher acknowledges with thanks permission to reproduce material
from the following publications: *The Alternative Service Book 1980* © The Central
Board of Finance of the Church of England.
Celebrating Common Prayer: A Version of the Daily Office SSF © Mowbray, 1994.

Biblical quotations are from *The Revised English Bible*, Oxford University Press and
Cambridge University Press, 1989, unless otherwise indicated.

Text identified as D.C. in the Notes section is written by the author.

The publisher takes this opportunity to thank those individuals and
organizations who have given us permission to use and adapt material for
this book. Every effort has been made to trace the owners of copyright
material, though in a few cases this has proved impossible and we apologize to any
copyright holders whose rights may have been unwittingly infringed. We trust that in
the event of any accidental infringement, the owners of
the material will contact us directly.

British Library Cataloguing-in-Publication Data

A catalogue record for this book is available from the British Library.

ISBN 0–281–05111–9

Typeset by Pioneer Associates, Perthshire
Printed in Great Britain by
The Cromwell Press, Melksham

Contents

—— *Acknowledgements* ——

I am most grateful to the Archbishop of York, for
writing the Foreword, and to Armorel Willmot,
Rachel Boulding and the editorial staff at SPCK
for their patience and skill in bringing order
out of chaos.

——— *Foreword* ———

Donald Coggan's style is distinct, combining a crisp turn of phrase with bold descriptions whose alliteration makes them memorable. As one reads, one can hear him speaking. But like Peter, in the courtyard of the High Priest on the night Jesus was on trial, his accent gives him away.

For in those accents clear and still, one can also hear Paul speaking and, through Paul, Christ. Donald Coggan combines a vivid imagination, a life's work being a "sent man" and a scholarship which immerses itself in the Hebrew Scriptures and the Greek New Testament to produce an accessible life of Paul which, essentially, whets the appetite and makes one hunger for more.

A *tour de force* review of the doctrinal and spiritual content of Paul's letters, which could be a very tedious journey in other writers' hands, is given sparkle when juxtaposed against the personal and striking events in Paul's life. These, in turn, are set against a homely record of Jesus' life and the lives of his followers, right through to the present day. In so doing, this work makes Paul alive, in Christ, and supremely relevant for both the world and the Church of today. It embraces a message which interweaves both prophecy and wisdom, pulling no punches as it does so. To borrow from Donald Coggan's description of Paul, this may be a book small of stature, but it is big in mind.

Any writer would be rightly proud to produce such a wide-ranging piece of work. Publishing this book in his eighty-ninth year, Lord Coggan deserves a double accolade. When he describes Paul at the end finding himself "still only tiptoe-deep in the ocean of the love of his redeeming God" one suspects there is a humble portrait of the artist here as well as the sitter. Only tiptoe deep he may be, yet his pioneering work and ministry (from which I benefit immensely, in having him as my predecessor, mentor and friend) firmly beckons others to wade with him into a sea which is thoroughly Christ.

David Hope,
Archbishop of York

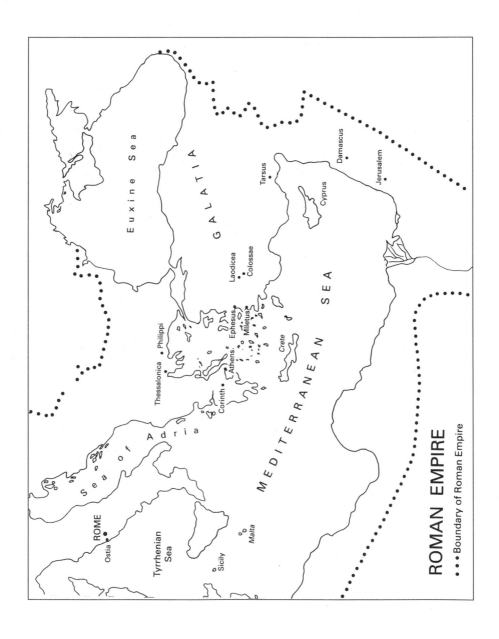

Euxine Sea

GALATIA

Tarsus

Damascus

Jerusalem

Cyprus

Laodicea
Colossae

MEDITERRANEAN SEA

Ephesus
Miletus
Athens
Crete

Philippi

Thessalonica

Corinth

Sea of Adria

ROME

Ostia

Tyrrhenian Sea

Sicily

Malta

ROMAN EMPIRE

•••• Boundary of Roman Empire

——— *Preface* ———

Early in 1994 I gave a series of midday talks in Winchester on the person and work of Jesus Christ. These appeared, considerably enlarged, under the title *The Servant-Son: Jesus Then and Now* (SPCK 1995). Early in 1996 I gave another series, this time on the apostle Paul. I welcome the opportunity of issuing the talks in an expanded form in this book.

The object of the book is clear. As the title indicates, it is an invitation to meet a man who has been a figure of world-wide influence during the last two millennia. To *meet* the man – is that possible? I think it is. To watch him in his home setting and in his withdrawal to the desert; to envisage him as preacher and pastor, as correspondent and man of prayer; to try to penetrate the meaning of his favourite phrase, "in Christ" – all this is to come into touch with a complex character, passionate, affectionate, very human. He exposes himself to us as a man of unruly temperament, learning, not without difficulty, what it means to take upon himself the yoke of Jesus, to become an apprentice to a Master who could handle him and teach him how to obey his calling.

A great many thoughtful people have shied away from the possibility of meeting this man. They have had no desire for such an encounter, for they thought of him as a bookish and rather crabbed person, a chilly mortal. I believe he was nothing of the sort. My hope for this book is that the reader will so meet Paul in these pages that, when he bumps into him in the life to come, he will say to the apostle, "I think we have met before." And the apostle will embrace the reader and with a huge smile will say: "So you were a man/woman in Christ too! Glad to meet *you*."

The limitations of this book are obvious. It does not claim to be an introduction in the technical sense of that word, still less is it a commentary on Paul's letters (that would take a series of volumes). There is a wide range of matters which are interesting but for which there is no room. For example, what do we mean when we speak of Galatia? How many letters can be seen in the Corinthian correspondence? Was the apostle the author of the letters to Timothy and Titus in whole or in part? All these and a dozen other questions can wait. What we want to do is to meet the man, the man "in Christ".

I have not included a book list for further reading – I want my readers to study Paul's letters, and the Acts of the Apostles, without distraction. When they have dug deep here, they may wish to explore the huge literature which has appeared, and continues to appear, about the man and his letters. First things first!

As to the readers of this book: I have had in mind individuals who want to understand the man and (conceivably) to meet him, and groups meeting for study in homes or parish rooms. Such individuals or groups should have a modern version of the Bible at hand. I have worked on *The Revised English Bible* (Oxford University Press and Cambridge University Press, 1989), though I have felt free to offer my own renderings occasionally.

I have concluded each chapter with some prayers, for prayer was a vital constituent of Paul's discipleship and it is in a spirit of prayer that we best understand him. At the end of the book, I have added some questions for further study.

Donald Coggan
Winchester

The Man and his World

"I am a Jew from Tarsus in Cilicia, a citizen of no mean city."

Acts 21.39

———

Israelite by race . . . a Hebrew born and bred . . .

Philippians 3.5

———

The commandant came to Paul and asked, "Tell me, are you a Roman citizen?" "Yes", said he.

Acts 22.27

———

. . . penniless, we own the world.

2 Corinthians 6.10

———

I bear the marks of Jesus branded on my body.

Galatians 6.17

———

I was, and am . . . an insatiable devourer of biographies. I am fascinated by the question of how other earthly wayfarers experienced their joys on this planet and how they coped with their problems.

Helmut Thielicke[1]

I have a deep love, amounting almost to an obsession, for the reading of biography and autobiography. Among recent books I mention Roy Jenkins' *Life of Gladstone* (Macmillan, 1995), John Dancy's *Life of Walter Oakeshott – "A Diversity of Gifts"* (Michael Russell, 1995) and Sarah Bradford's *Elizabeth* (William Heinemann, 1996).

Gladstone died a century ago (1898), but Jenkins had plentiful material on which to draw: previous biographies of the great man, his diaries, his speeches as recorded in Hansard and so on. Walter Oakeshott, headmaster of Winchester College, Rector of Lincoln College, Oxford, and Vice-Chancellor of Oxford University, died in 1987. He was a close friend of his biographer, and John Dancy was able to call on a host of men and women whose paths had crossed with Oakeshott's over the years. There were excellent pictures, and records of his speeches and writings. Queen Elizabeth II is, thank God, still with us. Sarah Bradford, in undertaking to write the biography of a reigning monarch, must have felt herself almost overwhelmed by the mass of material at her disposal: radio and television recordings, press cuttings, previous *Lives* as well as the contributions of people across the world who have had contacts with the Queen during her long reign of over 40 years.

Compared with such biographies as these, it would be impossible to write a Life of Saul of Tarsus (Paul the apostle). We have no recordings of his voice, no photos, no press cuttings, no books of sermons or addresses. We do not know the date of his birth, nor of his death, though we can make reasonably accurate guesses to within a few years. It is not the purpose of this book to attempt the impossible. It would be a fool who thought he could be a "biographer" of Paul, except in the most general sense. And yet the title of this book is *Meet Paul*. Is not a meeting even more impossible? A meeting involves a looking into the eyes of the person concerned, some sensing of his heartbeat, some intimacy of knowledge.

It is because I believe that, in a deep sense, this is possible; because in the course of my life I have almost entered into a friendship with him and have known many others who have done so at a far deeper level than I have; because I covet for others this intimacy with a man of immense stature, that I have attempted this book. There is another reason: Paul has been – and is – one of the most misunderstood figures who have appeared on the stage of world history. He has been the victim of some of his would-be expositors, who have hung conclusions on texts which cannot bear their weight and, in doing so, have converted this man of tender compassion and pastoral care into a rigid dogmatist whose frown, under their exposition, has scared people to death.

What material have we to draw on? The field is not so barren as we might first think when we compare first-century writers with modern ones. We have at least four sources: Paul's correspondence; Luke's contribution in the Acts of the Apostles; a strangely vivid description in the Acts of Paul and Thecla; and the experience of men and women who, down the centuries, have nourished their spiritual lives on the Pauline letters. Let us look at these sources in turn:

Paul's correspondence. Though I shall refer from time to time to the pastoral epistles (1 and 2 Timothy and Titus), these references will be comparatively rare. Though these three letters are of great value, they have to do mainly with matters of Church order and discipline (for example, how to behave oneself in the Church of God (1 Timothy 3.15)), and many scholars hold that, at least in part, they come from a later hand than Paul's. Some scholars, too, hold that letters such as Ephesians and Colossians bear the marks of a disciple rather than of the master. One may be allowed to say that, if this is so, the disciple reflected the master's mind with a faithfulness and an insight which are commendable.[2]

One can tell a great deal about a man by the letters he

writes. Paul had no inhibitions about exposing his heart as well as his mind in the letters he wrote to individuals and to groups of disciples in such places as Corinth and Rome. In one letter he shows his concern for the welfare of a runaway slave (Philemon); in others he shows his care for and gives his directions to groups of disciples who constitute the churches he had visited (in such places as Corinth and Galatia) or intended to visit (Rome). There are touches of asperity from time to time, more often touches of love and hope, as we shall see.

The letters cover the period of his intense missionary activity. Did he ever reach Spain? He wanted to go there. Did he write a letter to the Spaniards and other letters which got lost? Quite likely. Shall we ever find them? Probably not. We long for more, but we have quite enough to gain a picture of the man as he was. They are self-revelatory.

Luke's contribution in the Acts of the Apostles. The two men, Paul and Luke, were close friends. Paul refers to his "dear friend, Luke, the doctor" (Colossians 4.14). We can imagine him calling on the skill of his travel companion when his body suffered from the strains of constant travel and cruel persecution. (How much, one wonders, does Paul's favourite description of the Church as the *Body* of Christ, its Head, owe to Luke's explanation to Paul of the miracle of the human anatomy?)

Luke writes as an unashamed admirer of his friend, though he does not disguise Paul's weaknesses. The so-called "we" sections of the Acts, those passages where Luke writes in the first person plural, give us some incomparably vivid descriptions of Paul and his world; you get to know a man, warts and all, when you have travelled with him by donkey and by boat or on foot. The letters of Paul himself and the very considerable chapters which Luke devoted to Paul's travels and trials must be read side by side. They interweave.

4

The Acts of Paul and Thecla. This second-century description of Paul is, in part, so unflattering as to suggest its authenticity. It runs: "A man small in size, with meeting eyebrows and a rather large nose, bald-headed, bow-legged, strongly built, full of grace; for at times he looked like a man, and at times he had the face of an angel."[3]

Paul's correspondence and Luke's contribution are of considerable weight, with a touch of colour added by the unknown author of the Acts of Paul and Thecla. There is a fourth source more difficult to describe, but one of great importance when we are asking whether we can "meet Paul" with any degree of intimacy, whether we can cross the centuries and hear his heartbeat. During those centuries, and today in increasing numbers, men and women like ourselves have come to be "in Christ", as Paul was "a man in Christ" (see also Chapter 6 of this book). They have become limbs in the Body of Christ as Paul himself was incorporated into that Body. They would dare to say that they have "met" Christ, or, to put it more accurately, he has "met" them, for he is the *living* Christ. Church militant and Church triumphant are one, one in Christ.

Generation after generation, such people have found themselves being enlightened and nourished by the story of this man Paul and, above all, by his letters. He, being dead, yet speaks, and speaks with great power. As they meditate prayerfully on his writings, they find that they are receiving something which is more than intellectual enlightenment. They are being spiritually fed, equipped for service, made sensitive to the intimations of God's Spirit through the writings of this first-century disciple of Jesus. The fellowship of the Church is the organ of insight into God's truth. One of the main agents of that insight, in the ongoing life of the Church as a Body and of individual members thereof, is this man Paul. We meet him as, illuminated by the Spirit, we weigh up his writings and become obedient to their message.

This "man in Christ", this slave of Christ, this apostle, when he wrote his letters was dealing with local needs. His writings have proved to have a vital relevance to the needs of succeeding generations – a miracle indeed. This means that when we approach his letters we need not only intellectual attention, but also spiritual openness, for these writings can become to us a word of God which is "alive and active", cutting "more keenly than any two-edged sword", discriminating "among the purposes and thoughts of the heart" (Hebrews 4.12).

Let us suppose that you could step back from the end of the twentieth century into the middle of the first, and that on your travels in Asia Minor one day you came face to face with Saul of Tarsus. What sort of man would you meet? "Small of stature" – the Latin word *paulus* means "little", though in Jewish history the name Saul has about it a touch of royalty. (Is there a hint of Paul's life story here? Has humility taken the place of pride?) Every inch of him speaks of his Jewishness (see pp. 9–10). It might well be that the first impression that you got was of his sheer physical toughness. Look at the colour of his skin: sun-tanned and weather-beaten. Anyone who has crossed the Anatolian plains of Turkey (known to Paul as Galatia) will understand why the stock-breeders there wear sheepskins: to protect them from winds which cut like a knife and, in the summer, the sun which burns like a fire. His face is marked with deeply etched lines, etched by the weather, by pain and persecution, by long, deep thought, by concern for those on whose behalf he undertakes those endless journeys. He writes to his friends at Corinth: "overworked ... imprisoned ... scourged ... many a time face to face with death. Five times the Jews have given me the thirty-nine strokes; three times I have been beaten with rods; once I was stoned; three times I have been shipwrecked, for twenty-four hours I was adrift on

6

the open sea." (2 Corinthians 11.23-25) The list goes on. Anyone who can stand that and survive is tough. As Paul talks with you he might doff his coat and show you the scars, the honourable scars, which he had gained in service for his Lord: "I bear the marks of Jesus branded on my body" (Galatians 6.17).

If he was tough physically, Paul was tough in character, too. Luke tells a couple of stories about him which illustrate this. On the first occasion (Acts 16.19-40) he ran into serious trouble in Philippi and found himself the centre of an attack by the mob. Stripped and flogged by order of the magistrates, he was flung into prison and his feet were held fast in the stocks. There was an earthquake, the fetters were unfastened and the magistrates ordered their officers to release Paul and his friend Silas. The jailer reported the order to Paul. "Now you are free to go in peace." Did Paul meekly accept his freedom and go on his way? Not at all. "We are Roman citizens," he cried. "They gave us a public flogging and threw us into prison without trial. Are they now going to smuggle us out by stealth? No indeed! Let them come in person and escort us out." And come the magistrates did; they apologised and then escorted them out.

On another occasion, Paul was in trouble again, this time in Jerusalem (Acts 22.22-23.5). He escaped a flogging only because he made it clear that he was a Roman citizen. The commandant, realising that he himself would be in hot water if he maltreated such a person, ordered the chief priests and the entire Council to assemble and then gave Paul the opportunity to address them. Paul had only uttered a few words when the high priest ordered his attendants to strike him on the mouth. Stung by this action, Paul retorted: "God will strike you, you whitewashed wall!" True, he apologised when he realised that he had addressed these words to the high priest. (Was he suffering from eye trouble and so could not see the dignitary's robes?) Both these incidents depict a tough

7

man with a temper which could easily be aroused. No mealy-mouthed man here! No plaster saint!

He could be tough, too, with his fellow Christians when he thought they were in the wrong (Acts 15.36–40). Barnabas wanted to take John Mark with them on a visit to various churches in different centres. Paul thought otherwise, for he felt keenly the fact that John Mark had once deserted them. There was a sharp dispute and Paul chose Silas as his companion. We do not know the rights and wrongs of the case, but the incident casts a light on one facet of Paul's character.

When he felt that the integrity of the gospel was at stake, he could be very tough (Galatians 2.11ff.). He himself tells us of one occasion when he opposed Peter to his face because it seemed clear that Peter was reneging on a truth which previously he had seen and welcomed. Peter had grasped the fact that the question of who were his meal companions did not matter; oneness in Christ transcended all divisions between Jewish and Gentile Christians. But when he found that some of the old stalwarts in Jerusalem wanted to maintain such divisions, Peter joined them and accepted their course of action. Paul saw at once that this matter, which superficially seemed of such small significance, actually raised an issue of fundamental importance: was Christianity to become a subsidiary branch of Judaism or was it to be a faith open to the world, irrespective of human differences? "I opposed him to his face because he was clearly in the wrong" (Galatians 2.11).

Paul knew how to aim his punches. "You stupid Galatians," he wrote. "You must have been bewitched . . . Can you really be so stupid? You started with the spiritual; do you now look to the material to make you perfect?" (Galatians 3.1ff.). Paul was a Mr Valiant-for-Truth.

His toughness was a toughness born of love and tempered by love. Paul has much to say in his letters about the love of God – and he is not theorising: "Through the Holy Spirit he

8

has given us, God's love has flooded our hearts," he wrote (Romans 5.5). Considering the opposition which he met, the soil of his character might have become hard and barren, but God had been at work in him, melting the frozen, warming the chill, bending the stubborn heart and will. That love over-flowed into his relationships with the people he met. There are very tender passages in his letters. Now he is like an expectant mother: "I am in labour with you all over again until you come to have the form of Christ" – and that is written to the "stupid Galatians"! (Galatians 4.19) Now he is like a father: "You may have many thousands of tutors in Christ, but you have only one father; for in Christ Jesus you are my offspring, and mine alone, through the preaching of the gospel" – and that is writ-ten to the Corinthians (1 Corinthians 4.15), many of whom, living in that demoralised city, had disgraced the man who had begotten them. He loved them still. Now he is a patriot, grieved by the blindness of the nation from which he himself came, his "heart's desire and prayer being for their salvation" (Romans 10.1). He declares: "I would even pray to be an outcast myself, cut off from Christ, if it would help my brothers, my kinsfolk by natural descent." (Romans 9.3) Paul was controlled by the love of Christ; he was a man driven by love.

Toughness and love are not mutually exclusive. They can be complementary. Paul was big enough to accommodate them both. The man's body may have been small, but his heart was big.

Young Saul of Tarsus had much going for him. Though he was born in a pagan city, Tarsus, in what we should now call South-East Turkey, he came of a deeply religious Jewish family. He was never ashamed of his origins: "circumcised on the eighth day, Israelite by race, of the tribe of Benjamin, a Hebrew born and bred; in my practice of the law a Pharisee" (Philippians 3.5). If asked to spell out what membership of the Jewish race meant to him, he might well reply in the words he wrote to the Romans later in his life:

My brothers, my kinsfolk by natural descent . . . descendants of Israel, chosen to be God's sons; theirs is the glory of the divine presence, theirs the covenants, the law, the temple worship, and the promises. The patriarchs are theirs, and from them by natural descent came the Messiah (Romans 9.3ff.).

What a heritage! He gloried in it.

From his mother's knee he had learnt of a God at once righteous and loving, of a divine Law given for mankind's total welfare, of a people designed to be God's agents in the world, of a future age when God's will would be universally done. Sabbath by Sabbath, he had gone to the synagogue, the local centre of worship, education and administration of justice. He had shared, with childish delight burgeoning into adolescent and adult appreciation, in the annual great festivals, and from time to time – could he ever forget the thrill? – he had gone up to Jerusalem, the centre of it all, the "navel of the world" (Psalm 48.2). Bewitched by its magnificence, he had marvelled not only at its position and massive size, but at the ministration of the priests and the teaching of the pundits. "Hear, O Israel: the Lord is our God, the Lord our one God; and you must love the Lord your God with all your heart and with all your soul and with all your strength." (Deuteronomy 6.4–5) That seemed to him to be the essence of it all.

If Judaism was the very foundation of the making of young Saul, there were other influences at work in him. The air he breathed every day was pagan air. Tarsus was a pagan city, with a university at its heart, part of the great Roman world. Its atmosphere was imbued with the influences of Graeco-Roman culture, which had given to the world a rich contribution of literature, art and knowledge. It had at its core a question mark, an avid desire to know, to enquire, to find out. The worship of idols abounded – temples, altars and offerings to "gods many and lords many" (1 Corinthians 8.5, AV) and to the

Emperor himself – but it was a weary polytheism and its efficacy was widely questioned by the more intelligent members of society. The question-mark at the centre of this culture was often accompanied by a heartache, a wistfulness and a yearning for fuller truth and greater light.

A sensitive boy growing up in that world, nurtured in a conservative, God-centred, Jewish home and yet surrounded by an atmosphere of liberal culture, Saul must from early days have been conscious of tensions which at times were acute. The local gymnasium, with its emphasis on the body and its beauty, and the local lecture halls, with their stress on mind and intellectual achievement, held an attraction which sometimes clashed with the religious and ethical conservatism – some would have called it stand-offishness – of the home where the exclusive worship of the God of Abraham, Isaac and Jacob was absolutely central. The teachers in the university of Tarsus had a very different world-view from the teachers in the Temple at Jerusalem. What, for example, was the relation between the gods and goddesses of the pagan world and the One God who reigned in lonely majesty yet cared deeply for his creatures' welfare? Was Yahweh just one more god to be added to an already overcrowded pantheon? The very idea made Saul's family shudder; to mention such a thing was blasphemy. And yet . . . ?

The problem was exacerbated by the ease of world travel in the first century. "Ease" in such a connection is a comparative term. The modern traveller, accustomed to journey by jet, grumbles if his plane is half an hour late after a transatlantic flight. If he doesn't like the sea, he crosses the Channel by the tunnel. In the first century, journeys were made by foot or by donkey or, at best, by horse. As for sea travel, the Mediterranean was mostly closed for the winter months, because the risks of travel by boat were too great. (For an example of such risks, we have only to read Luke's brilliant description of a shipwreck in Acts 27.) Even Rome could not lessen the storms, but travel in the first century was easier than in previous times, because the empire's overall rule had done much to rid the seas of pirates. Of course, there were still perils from such marauders, but they had been largely reduced. The "immense majesty of the Roman peace" was a reality which, when Paul the apostle later went on his mission, made his work easier, as did the network of roads which Rome built across its vast empire.

Ease of travel facilitated the cross-fertilisation of ideas. Young Saul, travelling from Tarsus to attend some great festival in Jerusalem, would have found himself exposed to pagan ideas and influences on his journey. Many a city at a crossroads of the Roman world was the focus for travellers hawking a wide variety of intellectual and religious wares. Jews and Gentiles rubbed shoulders with one another in the interests of commerce, but the exchange of ideas and ideologies must have been almost as heated as the buying and selling. The lands around the Mediterranean basin were seething with religions ancient and modern, with philosophies and cults new and old: a heady atmosphere for a Jewish boy to inhale.

Those visits to Jerusalem did much to deepen Saul's Jewish faith. To sit at the feet of the greatest rabbis, imbibe their wisdom, worship their God and begin to understand the ethical implications of their faith – all this combined to strengthen the roots of his faith, so that it stood firm against the winds of paganism. Nor did he listen only to the recognised teachers of the Jewish faith, the acknowledged wise men of the calibre of Shammai and the more liberal Hillel. There were other teachers whose comparative youthfulness appealed to young Saul. It is not impossible that, on one or more of his visits to the Temple, he stood entranced as he listened to one young man, Jesus from Nazareth, much of an age with himself, teaching in the Temple courts. There would have been a freshness and an authority about the person and the teaching of Jesus which seemed to mark him off from the ordinary run of Jewish rabbis. He apparently set little store by many of the things which to them were most precious, and focused on the Father-God and on his reign in a way which combined depth and simplicity. His illustrations and the gracious way he put things were such that the crowds hung on his words. It was rumoured that he had great healing powers. Saul from Tarsus would not have known what to make of it all . . .

Saul knew that he was above the average, richly gifted, a born leader – people turned their heads as this young man went by and whispered to one another: "He is bright. He has a future. We shall hear more of him." There are hints in his letters that he knew the meaning of pride and that it was only later on that, in the light of Christ's cross, he came to "pour contempt on all his pride". There is an interesting story which depicts his gift of leadership and which Luke records in his story of the shipwreck (Acts 27). (True, the story comes from the later part of Paul's life, but such leadership as Paul showed does not appear out of nowhere, as it were. Heroism generally emerges from a long period of growth.) Paul had embarked on a ship bound for Rome. There were 276 people on board, including a centurion and a number of prisoners and, no doubt, wheat merchants with their loads of grain. At first, all went well; they could hug the coast. But in open water they ran into a severe and prolonged storm which threatened to break up the ship and drown crew and passengers. It was Paul who took charge. He addressed them all. He put courage into them when, hungry and frightened, they were giving up hope. The story has a happy ending: the ship was lost, but all lives were saved. The captain of the ship cut a poor figure. *Paul* was the man of action on that journey, a leader born and bred.

We have gone some way towards answering our original question about the possibility of conjuring up a picture of Paul and even of meeting him. There are other elements to be borne in mind: for example, in addition to his intellectual equipment, he was a man of *trade* (Acts 18.3), a tent maker. The Jewish rabbis insisted that to have a trade was an honourable thing, and Paul was to make the point, in his letters, that he depended on no one for his upkeep (see, for example, 1 Corinthians 4.12). So his life and teaching were firmly "earthed". He was no airy-fairy theorist.

Let us summarise our findings. We have built up a picture of a man small of stature, but big in mind; cultured and privileged in home and background; tough in body and in argument; hot-tempered and gentle in his relationships with people; presenting to the world as a young man gifts which might well develop into leadership in the future.

What was that future to be, and under whose command was he to serve his generation? There were fundamental issues to be faced before such questions could begin to find an answer.

Prayers

Almighty God,
who caused the light of the gospel
    to shine throughout the world
through the preaching of your servant Saint Paul:
grant that we who celebrate his wonderful conversion
may follow him in bearing witness to your truth;
through Jesus Christ our Lord.[4]

Spirit of God,
give us the toughness to hold to our task
and the tenderness to reflect your love;
through him who, for the joy that lay ahead of him,
    endured the cross,
ignoring its disgrace,
even Jesus Christ our Lord.[5]

Take, O God, the things in our past that we regret
    and the things for which we are glad;
and, by the miracle of your working in us,
use them, the bad and the good, in the making
    of characters
after the likeness of your Son, our Lord and our Brother.[6]

"I went off to Arabia"

"Tell me, Lord . . . who you are." . . . "I am Jesus, whom you are persecuting."

Acts 9.5

God's Apprentice

Title of the autobiography of Bishop Stephen Neill[1]

Whose service is perfect freedom.

Book of Common Prayer[2]

We shall never be safe in the market-place unless we are at home in the desert.

Basil Hume[3]

It is there, in *solitude* and *silence*, that the voice of God is heard; it is there that the river of prayer is born, that prayer which is the life-blood of the Church.

Olive Wyon[4]

We are indebted to Luke for our initial introduction to Saul of Tarsus. Luke, the author of the Gospel which bears his name, and generally recognised as the author of the Acts of the Apostles, was a doctor, a man of culture who was to become a fellow traveller of Paul on his journeys. He introduces Saul in two sentences and then, a full chapter later, gives a very careful description of his conversion and what followed it.

The two-sentence introduction has a significance far greater than its brevity might suggest: "The witnesses laid their coats at the feet of a young man named Saul. . . . Saul was among those who approved of his [Stephen's] execution." (Acts 7.58 and 8.1)

It was a bloody scene: the death by stoning of the Church's first martyr, Stephen. The Christian movement was making rapid advance – new disciples, some of them priests, giving their allegiance to Jesus of Nazareth. They soon found themselves in trouble, and the venom of those who opposed them centred on the person of Stephen. Brought before the Council, Stephen found himself invited by the high priest to defend himself. He did so at length. When he pressed his message home, it "touched them on the raw, and they ground their teeth with fury. . . . they made a concerted rush at him, threw him out of the city, and set about stoning him." (Acts 7.54ff.) They had to strip – it was hot work gathering the stones and heaving them at the battered body before them. Where should they lay their clothes? There was young Saul, from Tarsus. He obviously approved their action; they could see it by the expression on his face. They would toss their coats at his feet. He would take care of them until, their bloody work done, they could call it a day.

What was going on in the mind of Saul that day? Stephen, whom they were stoning, was no ordinary victim of the people's vengeance. He was a man with a vision. He saw the glory of God and the person of Jesus standing at God's right hand, *standing*, as if ready to receive him. Saul listened while Stephen

17

prayed. Those prayers of his reminded Saul of the prayers which, so his disciples had told him, Jesus had prayed as he was being crucified. Stephen called out: "Lord Jesus, receive my spirit" (Acts 7.59), as Jesus had prayed: "Father, into your hands I commit my spirit." (Luke 23.46) Stephen cried aloud: "Lord, do not hold this sin against them" (Acts 7.60), as Jesus had prayed: "Father, forgive them; they do not know what they are doing." (Luke 23.34)

Saul could never forget those words. Nor could he forget that face – the face of Stephen was like that of an angel. Those words, that face, haunted him in the hours of those nights when he could not sleep. Stephen, radiant in his awful death, was speaking to Jesus as if the Man from Nazareth were still alive and waiting for the arrival of the first Christian martyr. It didn't make sense. And here was Saul among those who were responsible for Stephen's death. As often happens when conscience gets to work and perplexity abounds, Saul gave himself with renewed vigour to the cause of Stephen's persecutors. No longer would he be a silent onlooker as he had been at Stephen's death. He would threaten the Lord's disciples; he would apply for letters "authorizing him to arrest any followers of the new way when he found men or women, and bring them to Jerusalem" (Acts 9.2). Illogical it might be, but throwing himself with total abandonment into the abolition of the Christian movement seemed the best way to stifle the doubts which Stephen's death had occasioned.

Then it happened. But what was "it"? The conversion of Saul of Tarsus has had many "explanations", varying from the psychological to the physical, as if such a happening could be explained in any such terms! Anyone contemplating the scene on the Damascus road would do well to take the shoes off his feet, for the ground on which he treads is holy. One thing is clear: *God* was at work in the remaking of a man whose life was to influence people across the world over the next two millennia.

What happened to Saul that day is generally taken as the classic example of a sudden conversion. I doubt the adjective. I would prefer a word like "climactic" to describe this crucial event. We learnt in the previous chapter something of Saul's background: the orthodox Jewish home, the influence of synagogue and scripture, of Temple and sacrifice, of worship and conceivably of contact with Jesus himself in his teaching ministry. Saul had listened in to the witness of the first disciples and glimpsed something, though he did not understand it, of the radiance of their lives. Stephen's death must have seemed like the last straw. How he wished he could eradicate that picture from his mind.

It was all mounting up, like a pile of tinder awaiting the touch of a flame, ready for a combustion. The incident on the Damascus road was that touch of flame.

On a wall in the church of Santa Maria del Popolo in Rome there is a picture by Caravaggio of Saul's conversion. Central to the picture is the horse from which Saul has fallen. Young Saul lies on his back on the ground, looking up. His arms are outspread, open, so they seem to say, to receive anything which God has in store for him – forgiveness, if that were possible, new life, new work? "'Tell me, Lord,' he said, 'who you are.'. . . 'I am Jesus, whom you are persecuting.'" (Acts 9.5) Had he, in persecuting the followers, actually been persecuting their Master? The enormity of it came rushing over him. The glory of the Lord dazzled him. They led him, blind and battered, unable even to eat, to the town. God had his man ready: Ananias, doubtful and frightened at first, dared to visit him. More than that, he called him "my brother" (Acts 9.17) – a lovely act of peace – and introduced him to the Christian community.

The sequence of events after this is not easy to determine. Saul spent some time in Damascus – he needed it! The community would no doubt have to be convinced that he was genuine; was his "conversion" a trap? He needed their friendship once

19

they were convinced; needed their love to mend his wounded pride; needed to worship with them (the breaking of the bread was already central to their spiritual life as a body of believers). With a young Christian's enthusiasm to share what he had recently found, he would also seize any opportunities that came his way, to "proclaim Christ". He came to grips with the Jews in Damascus as he proved to them the Messiahship of Jesus.

Luke tells of his introduction by Barnabas to a timid group of disciples in Jerusalem and of a plot to murder him (Acts 9.26ff.). Paul himself, in the earliest of his letters, to the Galatians, makes the point that when at last he did go up to Jerusalem, the purpose of the visit was not to seek the approval of those who were apostles before him, because he had divine authentication for his work! (Galatians 1.1) He "got to know Cephas" (Peter) and stayed two weeks with him (Galatians 1.18ff.). But that was three years later. The visit to Arabia, and the return to Damascus after it, seem to have taken place soon after his dramatic meeting with the Lord on the Damascus road.

"I went off to Arabia" (Galatians 1.17). The phrase tantalises me. If we have got our sequence of events roughly right – conversion, burst of evangelistic activity, plot to kill him, Arabia – I believe we can make sense of it.

Arabia: stretching away south and east of Damascus, land of sand and oases, part of the trade route which brought the treasures of one empire to the tables of another, land of plodding camels, tents and bitter blood feuds, of scorching sun and perishing cold, of immense silence and starlit skies; of fascination for intrepid travellers over many centuries. *Why did Paul go there?* No doubt, with his new faith burning in him, he would have sought to share it with the owners of the camel trains so that they, in turn, might share it with those who bought their wares. These were opportunities not to be missed, but such opportunities presented themselves infrequently. The desert is primarily a place of silence, where a man can think without interruption, where he can sort things out, where he can pray.[5] The desert is the place, apparently, where God *makes* his men and women, where he can speak and be heard.

Things happen when God meets people in the desert. Moses received his revelation of God at Horeb as he tended his father-in-law's flocks in the scrubland of the desert. He learned his painful lessons of leadership of a recalcitrant people in the long years of wilderness wanderings. At Sinai, that terrifying area of rock and thunder, during his lone stay on the mountain, he received the Ten Commandments. Amos, a sheep-farmer in the scrubland south of Jerusalem, learnt what it meant to become a man of God. Then, when his day of testing came and he found Church and State united against him, he was able to face such opposition with those immortal words: "I was no prophet... nor was I a prophet's son; I was a herdsman and fig-grower. But the Lord took me as I followed the flock and it was the Lord who said to me, 'Go and prophesy...'" (Amos 7.14–15). John the Baptiser did his work of preparing the way for the Messiah, not in Jerusalem but in the wilderness. The people had to come to him *there*. And Jesus of Nazareth fought his battles and determined the nature of his mission, not in a crowded town or a busy university but in the desert. The long story of the desert fathers and of the beginnings of monasticism bears witness to the fact that out of the silence God speaks and in the stillness makes his agents.

Paul knew that. Paul needed that. For *that* he went off to Arabia. He had much to sort out.

First of all, what had happened to *him*? What occurred on the Damascus road was a climactic event, a literal conversion in the sense that he had been going one way, and now found himself in reverse gear. He had been turned around. Looking back, it was as if he had been running away from God, turned round, and found himself face to face with the God who, in infinite compassion, had been running after him, chasing him.

Somehow, the person of Jesus was central to this change. As Paul was later to write to his friends: "the light which is knowledge of the glory of God" was "*in the face of Jesus Christ*" (2 Corinthians 4.6, author's italics). As, sprawled on the ground, with arms outstretched, Saul looked up, he saw no condemnation in the eyes that met his, only infinite love and concern: "You are hurting yourself in kicking against the goad" (Acts 26.14). What had happened to him that this arch-persecutor now found himself proud of the title "slave of Jesus Christ"? What had happened that his mind was now being reformed, his character transfigured and his perception so changed that he could see God's will for the thing that undoubtedly it was: "good, acceptable, and perfect"? (Romans 12.2).

His relationship with God had undergone a radical change. He had found peace. He could look up into the face of God and know that all was well. His anxious striving for a right standing with God had given way to thanksgiving, his flurry of good works to the rest of reliance on God. All that needed sorting out.

Secondly, the recent events connected with the presence of Jesus in Israel appeared to him to be unique and of immense significance. Saul, as we have seen, may have heard Jesus teaching in the Temple precincts – may even have met him. Whether or not he did matters little. As Saul interrogated the followers of Jesus, he learnt a very great deal about this Jesus: about his birth and early years working at his trade; about his public ministry, brief but packed with teaching and healing; about his crucifixion and, so his disciples maintained, his resurrection and appearance to many. God seemed to have been at work in Jesus' life in a way without parallel in history. He had raised him from the dead and, though his physical presence was withdrawn and human eyes could no longer see him, Jesus was let loose in the world. Saul had met him on the road to Damascus and the meeting had transformed him. His first question was: "Tell me, Lord, who you are." The voice answered, "I am Jesus." (Acts 9.5)

The Person of Jesus; here in the desert he must think this through. Who *was* the young man endowed with such gifts and yet ready to be obedient even to death, to serve and not to count the cost? Could he be described in purely human terms or was he human indeed but so much more than that? Was his coming the great watershed of human history? Perhaps Saul would never be able to give a neat answer to these questions, but the desert would at least give him the opportunity to face them until the time came for him to set out on his world mission to proclaim his message.

Thirdly, the voice that spoke to him on the Damascus road had asked the question: "Saul, Saul, why are you persecuting me?" (Acts 9.4) He might well have replied: "I'm not persecuting you, Lord. I'm persecuting your disciples." He made no such reply, but the form of the question puzzled him. Was there such an intimacy, such an unbreakable unity, between Jesus and his followers that it was not possible to persecute the friends without, *ipso facto*, persecuting and hurting Jesus himself? Was it rather like the relationship between head and body – if you hurt a limb, that hurt is registered in the head, which suffers with it? Saul, out there in the desert, did not know that he was later to become a close friend of the medical man, Luke, who would explain the interconnectedness of Body and members. However, it may well be that Paul's great doctrine of the Church as the Body of Christ was born as he faced the question put to him at his conversion: "Why are you persecuting *me?*" He needed time and the silence of Arabia to sort it all out.

Fourthly, what was to be his relationship, as a follower of Jesus, to the religion in which, from childhood, he had been brought up? He realised with joy that God had entered into a covenant-relationship with Israel, had given his people the law, the Temple, the promises and the patriarchs. Indeed, it was through their line that the Messiah was to come (Romans 9.3–5). Saul was himself "an Israelite by race . . . a Hebrew born and bred", more than that, "a Pharisee" (Philippians 3.5). Was he now to abandon the faith of his forefathers, to turn his back on all that Judaism had meant to him? Never! In becoming a Christian he did not reject the old faith. Rather, he saw it as the bud from which the flower of the new emerged. On his travels around the Graeco-Roman world he would go first to the synagogues and share his faith with those who worshipped there. Indeed, as they read their Scriptures he would seek to help them realise that what those Scriptures foreshadowed Jesus in his coming and in his passion fulfilled. With his Jewish brothers and sisters he would share his new-found insights or, as he would prefer to see it, the revelation of life and liberty which God had given him in the person of Jesus, the Messiah. Only when he had discharged that duty (whether they would receive it or not), would he go to the non-Jews. But he would not seek to hide the fact that the "gain of gaining Christ Jesus my Lord" (Philippians 3.8), of finding himself in union with him, had altered the whole picture for him. Hitherto his religious activities – and they were many and vigorous – had been the basis of his hope Godwards: "I outstripped most of my Jewish contemporaries by my boundless devotion to the traditions of my ancestors" (Galatians 1.14). He had much to boast of, but there, precisely, was the trouble: pride in achievement, piling up his good works before God. On the Damascus road his pride was deflated; his good works could not establish a lively relationship with God. There, on his back, with empty hands outstretched, he could only wait for the mercy of God; in the divine pity lay his hope. Now, in the silence of the desert, he spent long hours viewing on the screen of his mind the figure of another young Man, his arms also outflung, but in love to the world – and to *him*. "The Son of God," he was later to write to his friends, "loved *me* and gave himself up for *me*." (Galatians 2.20, author's italics)

He had not abandoned the God of the Scriptures on which he had been brought up. There was continuity with the old, and the justice of God stood firm. The love of God, adumbrated, for example, with moving tenderness by some of the prophets, stood firm, but now with an enhanced glory. Worldwide in its outreach, limitless in its scope, concentrated and focused by the Figure on the Cross: "Then what can separate us from the love of Christ?" (Romans 8.35) There could be no doubt of Paul's answer.

Fifthly, what was to be his mission and his message? One thing was blindingly clear: the God who had revealed himself at the time of Saul's conversion was a God of infinite grace and compassion, a God of limitless generosity. He had revealed himself as such supremely in the person and work of Jesus of Nazareth. "You know the generosity of our Lord Jesus Christ: he was rich, yet for your sake he became poor, so that through his poverty you might become rich." (2 Corinthians 8.9) So Paul was later to write to his friends in Corinth. If that was true, it was of *universal* significance. That grace, that generosity, overrode all man-made barriers. ". . . in union with Christ Jesus . . . There is no such thing as Jew and Greek, slave and freeman, male and female" (Galatians 3.26, 28). Racial differentiation is at an end, the class barrier is down and the gender barrier is overcome. "It is through faith that you are all sons of God in union with Christ Jesus" (Galatians 3.26): *here* is the reality of God's revelation.

This was no invention of Paul's. It had become real to him on the road to Damascus, but he had received it as the essential faith of the early Church. He handed it on:

> First and foremost, I handed on to you the tradition which I had received: that Christ died for our sins, in accordance with the scriptures; that he was buried; that

he was raised to life on the third day, in accordance with the scriptures; and that he appeared to Cephas, and afterwards to the Twelve. (1 Corinthians 15.3–5)

It sounds like the outline of a creed, each clause being introduced by "that". Perhaps we have in these phrases the beginnings of the creed of the Damascus church.

For Paul, this was no formal series of articles of a creed, to be recited parrot-fashion. These short sentences were attempts to sum up events which had happened as a result of God's initiative, events which had radically altered the life of Paul himself, events of whose proclamation Paul was put in charge. He was to give expression to them in his letters with a wide variety of language: "God has caused his light to shine in our hearts, the light which is knowledge of God in the face of Jesus Christ" (2 Corinthians 4.6); "It was while we were still helpless that . . . Christ died for the wicked" (Romans 5.6); "through the Holy Spirit he has given us, God's love has flooded our hearts" (Romans 5.5). Here is doctrine made red-hot by experience, doctrine which can only issue in doxology and in a life of gratitude: "Thanks be to God for his gift which is beyond all praise!" (2 Corinthians 9.15) "From him and through him and for him all things exist – to him be glory for ever! Amen." (Romans 11.36)

Paul couldn't keep this revelation to himself. He had been taken hold of by Christ with a grasp so firm that he knew it was for life. God had touched him; his hand was on his shoulder. Paul was no longer his own man – he was God's slave, in a slavery so total that in it he found his own freedom. He rejoiced in that paradox which Augustine was to observe so perfectly: "whom to serve is to reign". Ananias had said to him when he introduced him to the church at Damascus (Acts 22.15): "you are to be his witness to tell the world what you have seen and heard". That summed up Paul's mission, and his time in the desert only served to clarify it.

To clarify it, and to begin to work out a *strategy*. The world was to be his parish, but the world was big and not easily traversed. True, the great Roman roads made travel possible and the (comparative) peace of Roman government meant that journeys would not be impeded by war. Also, the seas were freer of bandits than in previous centuries, but life was short and time was precious. How best could he fulfil his mission?

Paul realised that he, unlike his Lord, was very much a town man. He was at home in cities like Tarsus, Jerusalem or Ephesus, at home in circles of learning and commerce. It would seem right to aim for these places and leave others to concentrate on country areas. As he pondered these things in the desert of Arabia, he visualised (though somewhat vaguely) a map of the Mediterranean and the lands which bordered on it. He decided he must press west, ever westwards. In the long run he must reach Rome, the centre of the great empire. Who knows, perhaps he might even make it to Spain? Beyond that the geographers could do little to help him! His aim was to take the gospel "to places where the name of Christ has not been heard" (Romans 15.20). In the words of Clough, "Yonder, look, the west was bright", bright with opportunity for evangelistic work. He would plant churches, build up churches, care for them as a mother cares for her infants.

He was an *apostle*, which means "a sent man". He gloried in that word, as he gloried in the word "slave". He was not one of the original apostolic band, but no matter. The Lord who had sent the Eleven as missionaries into the world with a commission to preach and to heal was the same Lord who had called him so dramatically. He was "an apostle commissioned not by any human authority or human act, but by Jesus Christ and God the Father who raised him from the dead" (Galatians 1.1). There was a summons in that statement which brooked no denial.

To sum up: the period in Arabia enabled Paul to begin to sort out in stillness and in prayer:

what had happened to him on the Damascus road and in
    the events which led up to it;
the meaning of the coming into history of Jesus the
    Christ;
the inter-relationship of Head and Body, the fact of the
    Church;
his attitude to the religion in which he had been brought
    up;
the essence of his message and mission – the meaning of
    apostleship.

Paul went to the world as God's apprentice. God had taken
him in hand, to make him, train him and use him. His pride
had died, his boasting was no longer in his own achievements.
Now he gloried only in the cross of Christ. He had found a
Master and all his energies were harnessed in his service. Paul,
apostle and slave, could stand tall with God. He went into the
world with a song in his heart.

Prayers

Lord, temper with tranquillity
our manifold activity,
that we may do our work for thee
with very great simplicity.[6]

Thank you, Lord, for the pauses which help us to reflect –
      pauses in music;
      pauses in liturgy;
      pauses in sicknesses which put us on our backs
         that we may look up;
      pauses we resent till we see they come from you.
   Help us to remember we have two ears but only
         one mouth.
   Help us to listen;
      to obey;
      to rejoice.[7]

Lord, still me.
Let my mind be enquiring, searching.
Let my heart be open.
Save me from mental rust.
Deliver me from spiritual decay.
Keep me alive and alert.
Teach me, still me.[8]

For God alone I wait silently;
My hope comes from him.
                        Psalm 62.5

Preacher and Pastor

God forbid that I should boast of anything but the cross of our Lord Jesus Christ, through which the world is crucified to me and I to the world!

Galatians 6.14

. . . we were as gentle with you as a nurse caring for her children.

1 Thessalonians 2.7

I am jealous for you . . . for I betrothed you to Christ, thinking to present you as a chaste virgin to her true and only husband.

2 Corinthians 11.2

You are my own children, and I am in labour with you all over again until you come to have the form of Christ.

Galatians 4.19

You stupid Galatians! You must have been bewitched . . . Can you really be so stupid?

Galatians 3.1, 3

Choose, then: am I to come to you with a rod in my hand, or with love and a gentle spirit?

1 Corinthians 4.21

Luke certainly knew how to tell a story. In none of his writings do we see that skill better deployed than in the story of Paul's farewell to the elders of the Church at Ephesus. He tells it with considerable detail (Acts 20.13ff.). After all, he was an eye-witness of the events he was recording. Acts 20 is part of those "we" passages, where he writes in the first person plural, as a fellow traveller with Paul.

The circumstances were these: Paul and his party had arrived at Miletus, which was the port of the important city of Ephesus. He was in a hurry; he wanted to reach Jerusalem in time to celebrate the day of Pentecost there, if that were possible. Much depended on that "if". Irregularities of shipping and weather were many, and it is difficult for us who are accustomed to jet travel to appreciate how frequent and how severe were the hazards involved. He decided to bypass Ephesus; once in the city he would be sure to be surrounded by people eager to detain him, to hear his news and benefit from his teaching. Nevertheless, he wanted in some way to reach them, so he summoned the elders of the Ephesian church to meet him at the port – it was no great distance. He knew that he would probably never see them again, so he engaged in a review of his three years with them. He had spent far longer there than he did in other centres, his usual policy being to press on from city to city, in obedience to his urge to spread his message. His time at Ephesus had not been easy, and there were perils ahead for that infant church: "savage wolves would come in among them, not sparing the flock" (Acts 20.29).

The review ended, apostle and elders knelt down and prayed. Then "There were loud cries of sorrow from them all, as they folded Paul in their arms and kissed him; what distressed them most was his saying that they would never see his face again." (Acts 20.36–8) It was a moving scene. The apostle had endeared himself to the members of the church in Ephesus. They knew that he loved them with a sacrificial love. They loved him in return. They found it hard to wave goodbye as the sails of his ship filled with the wind and she moved off into the open sea.

It is worthwhile to look at Paul's review of his work in Acts 20, for it sheds much light on the man as preacher and pastor. It was set against a background of "sorrows and trials that came upon me through the intrigues of the Jews" (verse 19). No elaboration of that is called for, except to say that such things hurt more when they come from members of one's own race than when they come from outsiders. "I kept back nothing that was for your good" (verse 20) – there was no preaching to the gallery, no currying of favour by softening the message. "I delivered the message to you" (verse 20), like a man entrusted with a treasure to hand on. "I taught you, in public and in your homes" (verse 20) – we can see it all: the discussion in the market-place, where crowds would gather ready to hear what the latest newcomer had to say to them, and the weekly gatherings in the synagogue when the scriptures were read and the visitors may have been invited to expound. We can imagine Paul visiting the homes of the people, elaborating over a drink some of the points he had made the previous Sabbath, replying to questions put to him, sharing the faith which was dearer to him than life itself. "I set no store by life," he said; "all I want is to finish the race, and complete the task which the Lord Jesus assigned to me" (verse 24).

We shall come very shortly to examine the content of his message. Meanwhile we note two things: first, he maintains that he has disclosed to them "the whole purpose of God" (verse 27) – some claim! Perhaps he meant that he had not succumbed to the temptation to pursue some hobby-horse of his own to the detriment of other aspects of the gospel; he had maintained a balance of teaching which would, if followed, lead to a balanced life and character on the part of those who heard him. Second: he wants to assure them that he has been at pains never to be a source of expense to them: "these hands of mine earned enough for the needs of myself and my companions" (verse 34) – presumably by pursuing his trade as a tent maker. No one could ever charge him with making a profit from being a preacher-pastor! On the contrary, he believed in hard work. In pressing this lesson home, he gives us a saying of the Lord Jesus not recorded in any of the Gospels: "Happiness lies more in giving than in receiving." (verse 35)

We note that the message which he brought to Ephesus was centred in *God*. He is the great Reality, and it is Paul's consuming concern that people should be in touch with him as he has declared himself in Christ. Four words stand out as being the themes to which, during his years among them, Paul had returned again and again. His letters refer to the first three constantly (to the fourth less frequently). They are: *repentance* before God; *faith* in our Lord Jesus Christ; the gospel of God's *grace*; the *kingdom*. All four deserve our careful attention.

Repentance before God (Acts 20.21)

Repentance was no new concept to Paul when he became a follower of Christ. The idea was a constant theme of the writers whose scriptures he had listened to in the synagogue Sabbath after Sabbath from earliest boyhood onwards. The word was essentially a very simple one. It meant "to turn" or "to return". If you turned away from God you became an apostate, you turned from the light of following the one true God, towards darkness and death. Once that happened, to turn back, to turn round, to return to God was all that mattered. Which way were you facing, towards God or with your back to God? That was the ultimate question. For the prophets, the greatest tragedy that could happen to a nation or to an individual was that they should reach the point of "no return": "This people's wits are dulled; they have stopped their ears and shut their eyes, so that they may not see with their eyes, nor listen with their ears, nor understand with their wits, and then turn and be healed" (Isaiah 6.10), for a nation or a person, cannot be whole (healed) if they are facing away from God.

There is something stark about the very simplicity of this concept in Hebrew literature. It presents us with an uncomfortable either/or. Paul knew his Hebrew language, his Hebrew scriptures; he appreciated the sheer punch-power of their word for "repentance".

However, he also knew the Greek language and he knew the Greek version of his Jewish scriptures (the Septuagint). He appreciated the fact that the Greek word for repentance (*metanoia*) had about it a subtlety and a depth which was absent from the Hebrew word. *Metanoia* means a change of mind (*nous*), of attitude, of heart, which reaches to the depths of human personality. Such a change results in a different relationship of the penitent with God, with one's fellows, with oneself, with society, with the world at large. It is truly life-changing.

When a person repents, his relationship with *God* changes: he sees him no longer as a tyrant seeking to pull the rug from under his feet and condemn him. He is more like a shepherd seeking, at great cost to himself, to rescue the one lost sheep.

When a person repents, his relationship with his *fellows* changes: they, like himself, are the objects of God's concern, the most unlikeable having the possibility of rescue and newness of life, the makings of a character fashioned after the likeness of his Son.

When a person repents, his relationship to *himself* changes. Sinner though he undoubtedly is, he need engage in no self-hatred. Indeed, he may – he must – learn to love himself, not in the sense of cossetting himself or pandering to his own desires, but of seeing his almost limitless potential as a son of the living God, open to all his gracious and powerful activity through the Spirit given to him.

When a person repents, his relationship to *society*, to the

34

world at large, changes. This is God's world, of which he is a citizen – God's by creation and God's by redemption, for "God so loved the *world* that he gave his only Son" (John 3.16, author's italics). There is, therefore, a sacredness about the world; he must not abuse it. He will be ecologically aware, alert to the sin of damaging any part of this fragile planet. He will allow no favouritism of white over coloured, of male over female, of status in society, for God is no respecter of persons. At the cross of Jesus the ground is level.

For Paul, repentance had been shattering, blinding, climactic, and yet the experience on the Damascus road was only a beginning, the entry to a lifelong and developing change of mind and attitude. It would take him the rest of his life to explore the ramifications of repentance, and at the end he would find himself still only tiptoe-deep in the ocean of the love of his redeeming God. Repentance is a lifelong process.

Faith in our Lord Jesus Christ (Acts 20.21)

In one of the earliest of his letters, the letter to the Galatians, Paul allows us to share in the very heart of his experience of God as it had come to him in Christ. With monosyllabic simplicity he outlines it: "The life I now live is not my life, but the life which Christ lives in me; and my present mortal life is lived by faith in the Son of God, who loved me and gave himself up for me" (Galatians 2.20).

Central to those brief sentences is the word "faith". It is surely one of the most misunderstood words in the Christian vocabulary. It can, of course, be used (and rightly used) of a system of belief which is held by adherents of a particular religion – the faith of the Jews, the Islamic faith, and so on. It can be used almost in the sense of the word "creed"; the leader of worship might exhort the congregation to "confess their faith in the words of the Apostles' creed". Paul does not use the word in this sense. Nor does he use it in the sense of the opposite of reason – "I want evidence; you only talk about faith." With him faith is a lively word. It describes the entry into the enjoyment of a relationship between two persons, in his case the persons of Christ and himself. There is warmth in that concept.

Perhaps an illustration may help. When a person does homage to the sovereign – let us say, on becoming a bishop or a member of the Privy Council – he or she has to go through a little ritual which I for one have found to be meaningful, especially as I have always had a deep respect for the Queen. He kneels before her and, in a set form of words, professes his allegiance to her. As he does so, he holds up his hands, palms together. The Sovereign clasps his outstretched hands in hers. She says no word. But the action speaks for itself. It is as if she says to the person kneeling before her: "I accept your oath of allegiance. As you take up this new office, we are in on it together. In that assurance you may go to your work".

This is, of course, only an illustration, an analogy, but it has an immediacy, an intimacy, a warmth of relationship which is clearly conveyed by Paul's use of the word "faith" in his letters.

Perhaps the word "trust" suggests some of the warmth which could be felt to be missing in the word "faith" – "trust" and its close cousin in Paul's vocabulary, "hope". Confident hopefulness – does that describe it? In Philippians 3.1–11 Paul looks back over his pre-conversion days, his "zeal for religion, his meticulous observance of the law", which he had been taught. If these were the basis of his relationship with God, he was not "without grounds for such confidence", but this brought him no peace. He came to the point where he wrote off "such assets", counted them "sheer loss", "so much rubbish" when he came to "know Christ and the power of his resurrection". Christ "took hold of" him, his hands over Paul's in a grasp of assurance and acceptance. From that day he lived as a man overwhelmed by the generosity of God, a man in debt to Christ.

Paul never disparages the intellectual in a person's relationship with God. He only recognises its limitations. To him faith is much more than assent to a proposition or a series of propositions. A person may give his assent to a creed but at the same time be spiritually lifeless. "For those who receive the gift of salvation in faith, the fundamental human act is not the reception of the gift but *the entrusting of themselves to God* the giver of the gift" (author's italics).[1]

So far, we have stressed the individual aspect of faith – I cannot enter into the relationship on your behalf, nor you on mine – but it is within the fellowship of other Christians that this faith can flourish and bear fruit. We are members of a faith community, all (though at different levels of growth and development) recipients of divine mercy, all indebted for our very lives to God. Within that community the salvation process goes on. Paul, in a seminal passage, Romans 5.1–5, uses the plural "we", not the singular "I": "now that we have been justified through faith, we are at peace with God through our Lord Jesus Christ". The days of our rebellion are past. We walk in the light of God's forgiveness. We recognise that in his will lies our peace. "Your will be done" is the basic prayer of the Church, as it was of the Church's Founder, a prayer uttered not in a spirit of unwilling surrender but of total glad commitment.

Paul links faith very closely with grace, as we shall see shortly when we look at the third of the themes to which he comes back again and again in his ministry. Here we may note his linking of faith, and peace with God, and grace with "the hope of the divine glory that is to be ours" (Romans 5.2). For Paul that hope has a very specific content. No doubt he recalled the creation story of Genesis 1, with its great assertion "God created human beings in his own image; in the image of God he created them" (verse 27). That image, that likeness, had been spoiled by human wilfulness and disobedience, and the divine glory had been marred. The Christian hope is that it will be restored. God's activity in Christ has set in motion a life-changing process which arrests our degeneration. In the here and now a process of restoration is at work, and it will reach its consummation on the Day of the Lord. That being so, present sufferings take on a new aspect: "we even exult in present sufferings" because in the hands of a gracious God they can be productive of endurance and of Christian character. In that sphere of God's grace to which faith admits us, there is a progression which may be compared with climbing the rungs of a ladder. The lowest rung is suffering, but that can be productive of endurance, character and hope, a hope founded on God's overflowing love. Faith, even when it is as small as a grain of mustard seed, *can* move mountains.

Martin Israel puts it well:

> Through him [Christ] I can see how the corrupt human nature can be changed until it is sanctified, becoming holy in the very image of God. The change is a pure gift of God, the divine grace. All that is required is openness to that gift, a virtue that is called faith in the context of complete trust, such as a small child would possess but a sophisticated adult would be unable to comprehend . . .[2]

The gospel of God's grace (Acts 20.24)

Imagine, if you will, that there lies before you a page blank except for one thing: a downward-pointing arrow. Let it stand for the idea of God's grace (a major concept in Paul's experience and teaching). God makes the first move in any divine–human encounter. He takes the initiative because he is love, and love never hesitates to initiate the meeting. Now imagine that on that page there appears another arrow, this time pointing upwards. This represents faith, the human response. It may be very timid, uncertain, trembling, but it is enough to begin with. That upward-pointing arrow speaks of openness to God, like the openness of the arms of Saul of Tarsus as he lay on his back on the Damascus road, trembling and afraid. Where those arrows make contact, where divine grace meets human response, there is life, life of an entirely new kind: eternal life.

Luke, in his Gospel (7.41 ff.), records a story which Jesus told concerning two men who were in debt, one for a huge sum, one for a small. The size of the debt was unimportant. They were in the same boat: both in dire need, both penniless. It was well-nigh inconceivable that the moneylender would take the initiative and write off the account, but that, in fact, is what he did. "He *graced* them both" (verse 42). That is the word used for cancelling the debt. The same thing had happened to Paul. His debt had been huge: his persecution of the followers of Jesus, his share in the murder of Stephen and, above all, the obstinacy of his own pride and self-assurance. Fallen onto his back with nothing to offer except the sin from which he sought rescue, Saul could only await a divine initiative, a move from God to him. His faith was minimal; God's grace was maximal. The two arrows met and he was a man reborn. No wonder Paul preached the gospel, the supreme good news, of grace. It was from a full heart that he was to write to his friends at Corinth. "You know the generosity [grace] of our Lord Jesus Christ: he was rich, yet for your sake he became poor, so that through his poverty you might become rich." (2 Corinthians 8.9)

It is our own pride, our self-sufficiency, our dependence on our works, which are the main blocks to the inflow of God's grace. Pride is the ultimate sin. Luke, who had ample opportunity to know the mind and teaching of Paul, records other parables Jesus told which emphasise this point. The story of the two men who went up to the temple to pray, one a Pharisee, the other a tax-collector, is very clear (Luke 18.9-14). The Pharisee relied on his achievements, which went far beyond what the law demanded. The tax-collector could only pray: "God, have mercy on me, sinner that I am." (verse 13) The latter, not the former, "went home acquitted of his sins" (verse 14). He was open to the grace of God. The story of the two lost sons, commonly known as the parable of the prodigal son (Luke 15.11–32), ends with the ragamuffin son at the heart of a reception party and the proud elder son sulking on the doorstep. Here, perhaps more clearly than at any other point, meet the minds of the Master and of Paul, through the recordings of Luke.

In a lecture given by Alexander Men the night before he was murdered, that great Russian theologian-pastor spoke about God's grace:

> There is a power which Christ left on earth, which is given us for free: it is called grace. . . . You don't have to work for it, it's a gift. Yes, we must make an effort, yes, we must struggle against sin, yes, we must work for self-perfection; but we have to remember that we can't pull ourselves up by our own boot laces. . . . These efforts are only preparatory. This is the basic difference between Christianity and yoga: for yoga believes that we can reach to God and break in on him by our own volition. Christianity, on the other hand, says: you may work to perfect yourself, but you can't reach God until he comes to you. Thus grace surpasses the law.[3]

Proclaiming the kingdom (Acts 20.25)

The kingdom (or reign) of God was the central theme of the teaching and preaching of Jesus. Mark tells us: "After John had been arrested, Jesus came into Galilee proclaiming the gospel of God: 'The time has arrived; the kingdom of God is upon you. Repent, and believe the gospel'." (Mark 1.14–15) The age of salvation is inaugurated, the day of deliverance has dawned. A glance at a Bible lexicon will show how often the phrase "the kingdom of God" recurs in the story of the ministry of Jesus, but it will also show how rarely it appears in Luke's story of Paul's ministry. Luke, in the chapter we are examining

(Acts 20), records Paul as saying: "I have gone about among you proclaiming the kingdom" (verse 25). He does not elaborate the phrase. He states that, in Paul's ministry at Ephesus, he "spoke boldly about the kingdom of God" (Acts 19.8), and that, when finally he reached Rome, "he spoke urgently of the kingdom of God" (Acts 28.23) to the people who came to his lodging and, over a period of two years, "he proclaimed the kingdom of God and taught the facts about the Lord Jesus Christ" (Acts 28.31).

When we come to Paul's letters, we find him using the phrase in the sense of the sphere where God's reign is acknowledged, several times negatively and with a future ring to it: "thieves, extortioners, swindlers . . . will not enter it" (1 Corinthians 6.10); "flesh and blood can never possess the kingdom of God" (1 Corinthians 15.50). However, it is also a shining concept: "God calls you into his kingdom and glory" (1 Thessalonians 2.12) and, in a remarkable passage which speaks of the kingdom specifically as the Son's, Paul tells us that God "rescued us from a domain of darkness and brought us into the kingdom of his dear Son" (Colossians 1.13).

Paul, as a good Jew well acquainted with his Hebrew scriptures, would have been familiar with the writings of prophets and psalmists who declared "Your God reigns" and brought this conviction to their work as messengers of God. All that was part and parcel of Paul's inheritance, but now it was vivified and illuminated by the coming of God's Son into the human sphere. God's kingdom was the great reality. He must proclaim it, he must speak urgently of it. For the coming of the kingdom in its fullness the Church prays, and towards that fulfilment all creation moves.[4]

These four concepts, then – repentance, faith, grace, the kingdom – were at the heart of Paul's preaching ministry. To them he constantly returned. They constituted the essence and the dynamic of his message, precisely because they were the realities at the heart of his own life and experience. As he moved from city to city, he saw that where these four concepts were present, there was a lively Christian community. ". . . all I want," he said to the elders of the church at Ephesus, "is to finish the race, and complete the task which the Lord Jesus assigned to me, that of bearing my testimony to the gospel of God's grace." (Acts 20.24)

Entrusted with the gospel of God's generosity and with its declaration to the world, how does Paul describe his work as a preacher? I have examined this question in my book *A New Day for Preaching*,[5] but here I shall summarise: he is a *herald*, proclaiming the Lordship of Christ and, in so far as he must "proclaim" himself, doing so as the servant of those to whom he goes "for Jesus's sake" (2 Corinthians 4.5). He is an *ambassador*, representing his Sovereign, often to people opposed to him and suspicious of all that he stands for. "We are therefore Christ's ambassadors. It is as if God were appealing to you through us" (2 Corinthians 5.20). With a touch of wry humour, he says: "I am an ambassador – in chains" (Ephesians 6.20). He is an *evangelist*, in the straightforward sense of one who brings good news, good news which is focused in the Person of Jesus Christ: "he was preaching about Jesus and the Resurrection" (Acts 17.18). He was a *persuader*, one prepared to enter into dialogue with the interested enquirer, to reason, debate, persuade: "for the next three sabbaths he argued with them, quoting texts of scripture which he expounded and applied" (Acts 17.2–3).

These four words paint the picture of a man under authority, conscious of being on an errand for his King, prepared to argue his claims but never thrusting them down his hearers' throats. Paul was no preacher "six feet above contradiction". He was a preacher who was essentially a pastor, to groups of Christians scattered over the world, for whom he felt a deeply loving concern and for whose well-being as individuals and as groups he longed with all his heart.

We have been examining two quartets: the first, the essential emphasis of Paul's preaching – repentance, faith, grace, the kingdom – the second, Paul's description of his ministry – herald, ambassador, evangelist, persuader. In the light of these quartets we are bound to ask certain questions about the presentation of the Christian faith today. For example, can a preaching ministry which does not have these quartets at its heart be called a truly Christian ministry? A preacher who fails to stress Paul's Christo-centricity may be an able orator and a fluent essayist, but can he call himself a Christian preacher? Similarly, unless a Christian community sets high store by this concept, surely it is no more than a comfortable club whose members have a good time when they get together, or even take a leading share in the charitable work of the wider community. To be a church, it must be God-centred, filled with the Spirit, fed on the word and sacraments of the gospel, an army with banners.

A glance at the history of the Church during its first two millennia would seem to indicate that, when there has been a revival of its life, the influence of Paul and his teachings has been central to that revival. To put that negatively, when the Church ceases to proclaim the primacy of God's grace and on the power of faith, it withers and dies. Reduce the Church's insistence on the overwhelming generosity of God's love in Christ, and it becomes weak; its flame flickers.

These matters are of such importance as to justify our looking at two or three periods of the Church's history which would indicate that we are not far from the truth.

First, we have Augustine, saint and Bishop of Hippo (354–430). "His *Confessions*," as Henry Chadwick puts it at the beginning of his lovely edition,[6] "will always rank among the great masterpieces of western literature." For long years Saint Augustine was the object of the prayers of his mother, Monica. He was brilliant, dissolute, dissatisfied with the various philosophies which came under his review: "any book which lacked this name [the name of Christ], however well

43

written or polished or true, could not entirely grip me"[7] he wrote; "I found myself heavily weighed down by a sense of being tired of living and scared of dying".[8] Then:

> with avid intensity I seized the sacred writings of your Spirit and especially the apostle Paul . . . . The holy oracles now presented to me a simple face, and I learnt to "rejoice with trembling" . . . . In surprising ways these thoughts had a visceral effect on me as I read the "least of your apostles" [Paul]. I meditated on your works and trembled.[9]

The influence of Augustine's writings from the early fifth century down all succeeding centuries has been immense. What would have happened if he had not "met Paul"?

Next we skip a thousand years and consider Martin Luther (1483–1546), founder of the German Reformation, translator of the Bible, hymn-writer and controversialist. We may be shocked by his crudities and regret his sometimes unwise use of extreme language. We should certainly detest his anti-Semitism and the language in which he clothed his railings against the papacy. His greatness consisted in his stripping away of much that the Church had added to the original gospel, his laying bare of the essentials of that gospel and his insistence on the fundamental question of how a person can be right with God. Luther was appointed Professor of Scripture at Wittenberg, where his duties drove him to learn and expound the Scriptures as he had never done before. He began with the Psalms. In the autumn of 1515 he lectured on the Epistle to the Romans. "These studies proved to be for Luther the Damascus road."[10] So writes his biographer, Roland Bainton. As he grappled with the Epistle to the Romans, Luther said:

> I clung to the dear Paul and had a great yearning to know what he meant . . . . Then I grasped that the justice of God is that righteousness by which through grace and sheer mercy God justifies us through faith . . . . This passage of

Paul became to me a gate to heaven . . . . Luther had come into a new view of Christ and a new view of God. He had come to love the suffering Redeemer and the God unveiled on Calvary.[11]

We skip another 500 years and come to the Second Vatican Council (1962–5). Arising from the initiative of Pope John XXIII, its task was to renew the religious life of the Church and to bring up to date its teaching, discipline and organisation, with the unity of all Christians as the ultimate goal. The result of the Council was the opening of windows which the passage of the years had closed. The admission of the fresh air of the Spirit meant that the Church could never be the same again, however slow the implementation of some of the Council's insights may appear to those of us who want to speed up progress. How did these changes come about? A reading of the Decrees and Declarations of the Council shows how, again and again, those responsible pressed back through the controversies of the Reformation to the documents of the New Testament and, not least, to a re-examination of the writings of Paul. To use the words of Augustine, Paul's thoughts "had a visceral effect" on those who laboured at the Council. To use the words of Luther, they "grasped that the justice of God is that righteousness by which through grace and sheer mercy God justifies us through faith". A gate to heaven had been opened.

"Preacher and Pastor" is the heading of this chapter. The pastoral part of Paul's ministry is best understood through a consideration of his letters. To these we now turn.

Prayers

Paul preached:

Repentance

Holy Spirit of God,
    so work in us that
    we are no longer conformed to the pattern of this world,
    but transformed by the renewal of our minds.
    Where we are wrong, we repent.
Where change is needed, amend our attitude to others
    near us
        to the world we live in,
        to ourselves,
        to you, our loving God,
    until, by your mercy, we come to share the likeness
        of your Son,
    in whose name we pray.[12]

Faith

I kneel in prayer to the Father . . . that through faith Christ
may dwell in your hearts in love.

Ephesians 3.14, 17

Grace

I thank [God] for his grace given to you in Christ Jesus . . .

1 Corinthians 1.4

The kingdom

He rescued us from the domain of darkness and brought us
into the kingdom of his dear Son . . .

Colossians 1.13

Almighty God,
who gave to your apostles
grace truly to believe and to preach your word:
grant that your Church
may love that word which they believed
and may faithfully preach and receive the same;
through Jesus Christ our Lord.[13]

Paul at his Letters

"His letters", so it is said, "are weighty and powerful; but when he is present, he is unimpressive, and as a speaker he is beneath contempt."

2 Corinthians 10.10

I came to you, without any pretensions to eloquence or wisdom in declaring the truth about God.

1 Corinthians 2.1

Look how big the letters are, now that I am writing to you in my own hand.

Galatians 6.11

Here is my signature: Paul.

Philemon 19

With avidity I seized the sacred writings of your Spirit and especially the apostle Paul.

Saint Augustine[1]

"We have never had it so good." That is certainly true in the world of communication. We write a letter, put on the stamp, drop it into the red box down the road, and raise an eyebrow in disapproval if it does not reach its British destination next day or Pakistan in a week. If by chance it gets lost, we lift the phone and say aloud what we wrote in the letter. Now, thanks to science and the new world of fax and e-mail, our friend in Australia can see what we have written in England and respond forthwith. There are word processors, typewriters and copiers at the ready, too, so there can be no question that that was, indeed, what we originally said. The world is on our doorstep or, rather, on our desk. All this (not just fax and e-mail, but letter post, too) is, of course, very recent. The world of the four-wheeled horse-drawn post-chaise takes us back only to the eighteenth and nineteenth centuries. It is difficult to imagine anything much before that.

It is worth making the attempt, however. In the world of the first century it was, I suppose, possible to speak of a postal system. Rome had built a series of roads which linked the various parts of the empire together, and those roads could be the means by which messages were passed from one place to another, but, at its best, it was desperately slow, limited to the speed of a horse or a pair of human legs. Even this postal system (if so formal a phrase may be used) was open only to the great: Rome would utter a decree, and there was no quicker way to promulgate it than via those arteries of communication which were the roads. As to transport by sea, the Mediterranean was virtually closed for the months of worst weather, and there were the pirates to consider; their power had been clipped by Rome, but nevertheless they roamed the seas and imperilled the sailors and their cargoes.

For a man like Paul, for whom the world was his parish and in whose heart there burned a passion to reach the whole of that world with the love of Christ, there was no possibility of conveying his blessing like some modern Pontiff *urbi et orbi*. He had to use what means were available. There were two: personal visits (hence his constant travels) and letters.

In the sprawling Graeco-Roman world there was constant movement. From time immemorial, there had been the movement of the camel trains, bringing the luxuries of one country to supply the wants of others. Trade was international. As long ago as 900 B.C., Solomon had an agreement with the King of Tyre whereby he supplied timber for the building of the great Temple in Jerusalem. Lands as far away as India were in touch with countries in the Middle East and in Europe.

In addition, there was the commerce of ideas, ideologies and philosophies. Scholars would wander from one land to another, sometimes accompanied by their little bands of disciples, spreading their ideas and enlisting their converts. "Missionaries" abounded.

All such movement made correspondence possible. Paul was aware of this. He used his fellow Christians as his postmen, as they travelled the world on their lawful occasions. It was slow, it was uncertain, but usually it worked. And, of course, copies of the letters could be made – all by hand and not always accurately, but people were reached and that was his primary aim.

An interesting example of a circular letter is Paul's letter to the Ephesians. It begins: "From Paul, by the will of God apostle of Christ Jesus, to God's people at Ephesus . . .". In some manuscripts the words "at Ephesus" are missing, hinting that the writer's intention was to send a circular letter to the churches in Asia Minor. No proper names are mentioned in the body of the letter. At the end Tychicus is mentioned as its bearer, and Paul hopes that he will personally convey "news of us" and put "fresh heart" into its readers (Ephesians 6.21–22). Again and again it must have happened that the church of God at A would make a copy of Paul's letter before sending it on to the church at B. There is an interesting little note at the end of the letter to the Colossians: "Once this letter has been read among you, see that it is read also to the church at Laodicea, and that you in turn read my letter to Laodicea" (Colossians 4.16). This letter has, to our great profit, survived, whereas the letter to the Laodiceans has perished, but Paul wanted both churches to have the benefit of hearing both letters. How many of his letters were lost? We can only hazard a guess – and long for more!

There was no paper, as we understand the word, in the first century. The word "paper" comes from the word "papyrus", and we know what that was. Made from the leaves of a reed-like plant, rubbed smooth with pumice, it provided an adequate surface for the ink, which was made largely of soot, gum and water. (Vellum, a parchment made from the skin of a kid or lamb, was reserved for expensive work, not for everyday use.) Given a very dry place, such as the desert sands, papyrus had great powers of longevity. During the last hundred years or so, the study of the language in which the books of the New Testament were written has been greatly enhanced by the evidence of thousands of papyri, some of considerable length, some little more than scraps. They reveal that no special form of Greek was used for conveying the gospel. The message of God for the people was communicated in the language of the people, a fitting medium for the story of the One who "bore the human likeness" (Philippians 2.7) and who "pitched his tent among us" (John 1.14).

It seems to have been Paul's custom to dictate his letters. We know the name of one of his "secretaries": "I Tertius, who took this letter down, add my Christian greetings." (Romans 16.22) Paul, perhaps to show the genuineness of the letter or as a sign of personal interest and affection, adds: "This greeting is in my own hand – Paul" (1 Corinthians 16.21); "I add this greeting in my own hand" (Colossians 4.18). His message to the Galatians is even more interesting: "Look how big the letters are, now that I am writing to you in my own hand" (Galatians 6.11). It had been a tough letter, which some friend had had to take down. Perhaps a personal PS would help to show his care, coming as the letter did from one whose discipleship was very costly: "I bear the marks of the Lord Jesus branded on my body" (verse 17). And why the big letters, the outsize characters? Bad eyesight? Perhaps – and the light was probably poor. Or is there a half-humorous rebuke there? Is Paul saying: "I'm writing to children (in the faith); you will be able to read capital letters more easily than small ones."

Little did Paul ever dream that some of his letters would one day be part of "Holy Scripture", bound up with the Gospels and other writings as part of the Canon, translated into the best part of 2000 languages, commented on by learned scholars, meditated on by millions of women and men, a source of spiritual life through which the Spirit would bring encouragement, rebuke, direction. The letters were written to meet particular needs or crises; written to specific groups of people whose faces were familiar to Paul, or to groups which he hoped to visit on some future occasion. Two letters, the letters to Philemon and to the Romans, very different in kind, will serve to illustrate this point.

Philemon

The shortest of Paul's letters, that to Philemon, is the most personal. Philemon was a Christian of some standing in the community at Colossae. His slave, Onesimus, had run away. Paul is concerned about the kind of reception that Onesimus would receive at the hands of Philemon when, together with Tychicus, he returned to his master (see also Colossians 4.7–9). Would Philemon impose the severe penalty which a runaway slave would normally have received at the hands of his owner? Paul points out that there are other considerations to be borne in mind. Philemon is a Christian, but so is Onesimus. They are both members of the Body of Christ. In prison, Paul had become the spiritual father of the slave – he had led him to Christ. Now, Paul pleads, receive "my child . . . my heart . . . no longer as a slave but as more than a slave, as a dear brother, very dear to me, and still dearer to you, both as a man and as a Christian ... welcome him as you would welcome me" (Philemon 10, 12, 16, 17). It is a touching commendation, with enormous implications once one sits down to work them out. There is a twinkle in Paul's eye as he writes, too. He plays on the meaning of the slave's name: *onesimos* means in Greek "profitable" or "useful". Once Onesimus had *not* lived up to his name – he had run away, he was useless to his master – but now, all that was over. Onesimus had proved useful to Paul by looking after him in prison. Restored and forgiven, he would be useful once again, if received back into the service of his master.

The letter of Paul to Philemon is a delightful little note, full of Christian love and winsomeness.

Romans

The letter of Paul to the Romans is of a very different kind. It has 16 chapters (according to our very often unhelpful way of breaking up what is one document into chapters and verses), and is a substantial treatise, dealing with matters of immense theological and religious importance which get to the very heart of what the gospel is all about. It is written to a church which Paul had not founded – or even visited. As he writes to its members, he longed to visit them, to "come to you in a happy frame of mind and enjoy a time of rest with you" (15.32). At the beginning of the letter Paul tells them: "I want to bring you some spiritual gift to make you strong; or rather, I want us to be encouraged by one another's faith when I am with you, I by yours and you by mine" (Romans 1.11–12). Those are the words of a true pastor. If his visit to them could not take place for a while, he would write to them; the whole treatise is infused with pastoral care. God had given Paul the spiritual and intellectual gifts by which he would spell out to them the riches of the gospel. One day he will do that in person; now he will do it by letter. Romans is not a cold academic treatise, but warm with the great truths of Christian faith and pastoral concern. It is written with his heart's blood.

There is a phenomenon here which deserves some thought. Paul's letters, as we have seen, were written to meet the specific need of a specific group at a specific time: to answer questions which had been addressed to him, to warn of some special threat facing a group of Christians, or to rebuke those in danger of apostasy. And yet, these letters have been read by the faithful down the years, with a freshness which can only be ascribed to the influence of the Holy Spirit, the life-giver. They have met the needs of recently established churches in lands like Papua New Guinea and Africa (many of them unknown to Paul), and of young people undergoing fierce temptations in highly sophisticated, materialistic European and American cities. They have comforted and sped on their way old Christian warriors who have come to the edge of the river of death.

I have been searching for a word which will say what I have hinted at here. Is it the elasticity, the flexibility, the universality of the Pauline writings? I mean their applicability, centuries after their immediate purpose was fulfilled, to people in wholly different settings whose problems, at least to the casual glance, bear so little resemblance to those of the people whom Paul originally had in mind. Is this, in part, what we mean by inspiration? The presence and work of the Holy Spirit, in response to human need, using these ancient documents as the medium of God's grace? However we seek to define it, we are faced with an undeniable fact. If we cannot explain it with exactitude, we can thank God for it with total sincerity.[2]

In Paul we have a great theological thinker. The canvas on which he paints his picture is huge. He deals with the issues of time and eternity, of life as it is here and now, with its strange, complex mixture of agony and joy, and the life that is to come, with its mystery and glory. Paul is also an evangelist and pastor, concerned with founding new churches and nourishing Christian groups and individuals, babes in Christ and more mature believers. It is this combination of thinker and practitioner which accounts for Paul's greatness and which, incidentally, draws us to him.

He rejects out of hand any suggestion that, because God has acted towards us with almost unbelievable generosity, we are free to act as we will – more grace, more libertarianism! Such a conclusion is unthinkable. It is a prostitution of the mighty concept of God's love. There is an unbreakable link between religion and conduct; to this he reverts time and time again. He likes to remind his readers of their baptism: their descent into the water was their burial to the old life and the prelude to a life entirely new. He fears that perhaps his friends in the church at Rome had forgotten that fact: "Have you forgotten that when we were baptized into union with Christ Jesus we were baptized into his death? By that baptism into his death we were buried with him, in order that . . . *we might set out on a new life.*" (Romans 6.3–4, author's italics). He writes to the Colossians in similar fashion. He bids them not to forget their burial, nor their resurrection "through your faith in the active power of God, who raised him [Christ] from the dead" (Colossians 2.12). He tells them: "Therefore, since you have accepted Christ Jesus as Lord, live in union with him. Be rooted in him, be built in him, grow strong in the faith as you were taught; let your hearts overflow with thankfulness" (verses 6–7).

Nowhere is this union of doctrine and of the holy life put more strongly or more beautifully than in Paul's great letter to the Romans. Look at the architecture of the letter: the first eight chapters deal with the human plight, with God's judgement on sin and with his provision for our need; the meaning of faith; new life in Christ; baptism into him; and life in the Spirit. Chapters 9 to 11 deal with a specific problem: Israel and the Gentiles. Chapters 12 onwards deal with the Christian way of life within the community, and with service to all.

The connection is found in the opening verses of Chapter 12. The link word is "therefore", the first word of verse 1: "Therefore . . . I implore you by God's mercy to offer your very selves to him: a living sacrifice . . ." (unlike the offering of dead animals which occupied so large a place in Jewish devotion), ". . . the worship offered by mind and heart". Intelligence and emotion combine in the sacrifice. What will be the outcome of this whole-hearted offering? The answer is clear. It will be transformation, *transfiguration* (the Greek word is that which is used to describe the transfiguration of Jesus on the mountain in the presence of his three friends). The old pattern of life will be sloughed off, as a chrysalis sloughs off its old skin to make way for the emergence of the butterfly. The mind will be renewed; there will be clarity and daring of thought and imagination, and God's will will be seen for what it is: "good, acceptable, and perfect" (Romans 12.2). When we offer ourselves to God, we enter into a totally new life. There is a humility not known before (Romans 12.3), a new sense of belonging to one another in the Body of Christ (verses 4–5), and a desire to use to the full the particular gift which God has given, be it preaching, administration, teaching, counselling, leadership or helping people in distress (verses 6–8). There is also sincere love (verse 9). (Paul, in another letter, gives a whole chapter, 1 Corinthians 13, to the elaboration of the word "love".) The rest of Chapter 12 gives a most attractive picture of the transfigured life, with its overtones of mutual responsibility and care. All this emerges from a person's faith, his response to God's outgoing grace, the downward-pointing arrow of God's generosity meeting the upward-pointing arrow of human response (see pp. 38–9).

The letter to the Romans gives us a fine example of the interrelatedness of conduct and doctrine, ethics and theology, and life and religion.

When we turn to the letters to the Corinthians, we get a vivid and sometimes disturbing picture of a young church with problems. It enables us to get a fuller picture of Paul the pastor applying his doctrine to life as it is, with all its crudity and earthiness. No one who reads these letters could ever again think of Paul as a remote scholar cushioned against the facts of life! There is an intimacy of detail in the Corinth correspondence which is lacking in the letter to the Romans. Paul had not visited Rome when he wrote to the people living there, but he had stayed in Corinth for 18 months on his founding visit (Acts 18.11) and had got to know the people there.

These letters are of great importance: they contain the earliest written account of the institution of the Lord's Supper (1 Corinthians 11.23–26), the famous hymn to love (1 Corinthians 13) and the great chapter on the Resurrection (1 Corinthians 15), to mention only three well-known passages. But they also are important because they clearly depict some of the problems facing a young church in a cosmopolitan centre, and show us Paul as pastor, in his most intimate, caring relationship with his children in the faith.

Corinth was a great port and was beset by the immoralities which always mark the inflow and outflow of human life in such places. (A "Corinthian" means a dissolute or profligate person.) "God's church at Corinth, dedicated to him in Christ Jesus, called to be his people" (1 Corinthians 1.2) – it sounded fine, but as we read on, into the heart of the correspondence, we get glimpses of a people sorely tempted and not always triumphant. As their pastor, Paul had his nightmares. We need not read far into the first letter to discover what were the main causes of his concern:

Divisions, quarrels and party spirit (1 Corinthians 1.10ff.). There is a sense of shock in the series of questions and rebukes which Paul utters – there is a Paul party, an Apollos party, a Peter party and a Christ party at Corinth! He will have none of it. He tells them to remember who was crucified for them, in whose name they were baptised. Was it Paul? Perish the thought! They must return to the centrality of Christ, to their loyalty to *him*, and not split into factions.

Spiritual immaturity (1 Corinthians 3). Jealousy and strife among the Corinth community had led to lives lived on a purely human level; party spirit had resulted in spiritual immaturity. Paul longed to share with them some of the basics of the Christian faith, to feed them with the solids of Christian faith and practice. They could not take it, and he had to feed them, as mere babes in Christ, "on milk" (verse 2). He reminds them in his letter that the foundation of their faith was not Paul, nor any other human leader, but Christ himself. Now the building process was continuing, the building up of a spiritual temple, Paul warns them: "Let each take care how he builds" (verse 10).

Sexual immorality (1 Corinthians 5). Paul mentions one particular instance, that of a man having intercourse with his step-mother. The Corinthian Christians ought to have gone into mourning and disciplined the offender, but they only showed self-satisfaction. It might well be indicative of a general laxity of morals. He tells them to watch their step.

Lawsuits among Christians (1 Corinthians 6). To Paul it was a matter of scandal that a Christian who had a difference with a fellow Christian should go to law in a pagan lawcourt. Surely that difference should be resolved within the Christian fellowship, not outside it.

Matters such as these four presented themselves to Paul and called for his immediate attention. As a faithful pastor, he could not leave them unmentioned. There was, however, another side to the relationship between Paul and the members of the church at Corinth: *they* had questions which they wanted to put to *him*, subjects on which they sought his guidance. A large part of the second half of the first letter (1 Corinthians 7 to the end) consists of replies to questions which they had raised, and are introduced by the words "Now about".

Thus 1 Corinthians 7.1–24 deals with matters of *sex and marriage*. Within the framework of the principle that a wife's body is her husband's, and a husband's body his wife's, he differentiates between what he calls the Lord's ruling (verse 10) and his own views, especially about the question of a marriage in which one member is a Christian and the other member is not.

Verse 25 in the same chapter is clearly the reply to another question put to him by the members of the church. "About the *unmarried*", he begins. Again, it is his opinion that he gives. That opinion is affected by the stress of the time (verse 26) and his belief that the present age was drawing to a close. "For the world as we know it is passing away" (verse 31). (The anticipated imminent return of the Lord did not materialise – to the great surprise, we must assume, of those who were expecting to hear the trumpet-call of the second advent.)

"Now about *meat consecrated to heathen deities*." (1 Corinthians 8.1) A Christian goes shopping at the butcher's. He is offered a joint of meat which has already been part of a sacrifice to one of the many local gods or goddesses. The Corinthians want to know, should he reject it, or is it all right to buy the joint and eat it? Paul replies that such gods are nonentities, many as they are, especially in such a town as Corinth: "For us there is one God, the Father . . . one Lord, Jesus Christ" (verse 6 is the nucleus of a fine Christian creed). He lays down a principle whose relevance reaches out far beyond this particular matter of food; it is the principle of conscience. For a Christian who sees the truth that all idols are, in fact, nonentities, the matter of what he eats is irrelevant. He may have heard that Jesus said: ". . . nothing that goes into a person from outside can defile him; no, it is the things that come out of a person that defile him" (Mark 7.15). For another Christian, long brought up in the practice of idolatry, the issue is a very real one, however. The answer to the question is that you should never wound the conscience of a fellow Christian, even if, as in this case, abstinence from food causes you inconvenience or self-sacrifice.

"About *gifts of the Spirit*" (1 Corinthians 12.1). As we have seen, Paul was distressed at the party spirit which marked the life of the church at Corinth (1 Corinthians 1.10ff.). The church is not a collection of separate individuals at various stages of growth. Still less does it consist of a bunch of discordant groups. It is a Body, pulsating with one heart, with one Head, the various limbs interdependent, closely knit: the Body of Christ. Paul's doctrine of the Church is central to all his thinking; it is an essential part of his gospel. Here, in 1 Corinthians 12, in Romans 12.4ff., and again in Ephesians 4.4ff. he plays on this theme.

The church at Corinth was, potentially, a very rich church, not in material things – it had no buildings, financial assets or libraries, and probably few wealthy members – but it was richly endowed, with the gifts of the Spirit. When God gives he is not a niggardly giver ("so measureless is God's gift of the Spirit" (John 3.34)). God showers his gifts on his Church in rich profusion and in wide variety. Paul lists some of them: wise speech, the ability to put deep knowledge into words, faith, healing and so on (1 Corinthians 12.4–10). No one of them is for selfish aggrandisement, but "for some useful purpose" (verse 7), to "build up the church" (1 Corinthians 14.12). This being so, a Christian need not be jealous of a brother or sister who is endowed with gifts other than his own. His responsibility is to find out what is the particular gift, or what are the particular gifts, with which God has endowed him, to rejoice in them, develop and use them for the building up of the church. They may be gifts easily seen by all – speaking in tongues, for example. Paul himself was endowed with that gift and rejoiced in exercising it (1 Corinthians 14.18). However, he warns his readers that the use of the mind (14.15), helping the ordinary person to understand what is being said (14.16), decency and order (14.40), and above all love – these are the marks of a healthy, growing, worshipping community.

It is a pity that 1 Corinthians 13, rightly called Paul's "hymn to love", is printed in many Bibles as if it were entire of itself. Maybe originally it was, or perhaps Paul inherited it from another, early source, but it is part and parcel of chapters 12 to 14. The first verse runs right on from 12.31: "I can show you an even better way . . . I may speak in tongues . . . but if I have no love". And the end of chapter 13 ("the greatest of the three is love") runs straight into 14.1: "Make love your aim". Our chapter divisions are useful for purposes of reference; they do not always help in making the author's point clear.

The Corinthian Christians had written to Paul for guidance about the gifts of the Spirit (12.1); he took up the matter in considerable detail. There are minor passages in these three chapters (12 to 14) which puzzle us – the locals would have understood – but overall the message that Paul gives is clear: you have a lavish God; there is no need to live as spiritual paupers – grow up! "Do not be children in your thinking . . . be infants in evil, but in your thinking be grown up." (14.20) He reminds them that they are dependent on one another and should watch that interdependence with the sharp eye of love. In their worship they must keep in mind the outsider who may wander in, wondering what they are doing. Their aim should be to see him "fall down and worship God, declaring, 'God is certainly among you.'" (14.23–25) 1 Corinthians 13 urges Christians to let love reign, love which is not sentimental but practical and down to earth, never envious, rude, or selfish, greater even than faith and hope.

In 1 Corinthians 15 Paul spells out the meaning of *Christ's resurrection*. It is at the very heart of his message: "if Christ was not raised, then our gospel is null and void, and so too is your faith" (1 Corinthians 15.14). The risen Christ is "the firstfruits" of a great harvest (verses 20, 23), the guarantee of a future when, all enemies defeated, God will reign supreme (verse 28). Paul searches for illustrations by which he can convey something of the glory that is to be when the physical body, often the source of humiliation and weakness, shall give place to a "spiritual body" (verse 44). He refuses to be specific about what he means by that tantalising phrase, though "we shall wear the likeness of the heavenly man" (verse 49) has colours of glory in it. It is perhaps taken a little further in the passage in Paul's letter to the Philippians in which he looks forward to that consummation when Christ "will transfigure our humble bodies, and give them a form like that of his own glorious body, by that power which enables him to make all things subject to himself" (Philippians 3.21). This is not enough to satisfy our curiosity, but it is quite enough to steady a Christian's nerve and kindle hope, even when he lives in Corinth!

This great fifteenth chapter on the resurrection moves to its doxological ending, proclaiming that death is no longer to be feared, now that its sting has been drawn: "thanks be to God! He gives us victory through our Lord Jesus Christ. Therefore, my dear friends, stand firm ... work for the Lord ... your labour cannot be lost." (1 Corinthians 15.57-8). The next chapter begins, abruptly: "Now about the collection" (16.1).

The resurrection and *the collection* – a strange juxtaposition? Not at all. Men and women who recognise themselves as resurrection people, buried with Christ and raised with him, find they have a new relationship with their bankers. Their pockets are affected by their faith. Today the churches which are most deeply moved by the Spirit are those with fewest financial problems. Paul was organising a gift for the needs of the church in Jerusalem, and, in the opening verses of chapter 16, makes business-like arrangements for its collection and delivery.

"As for *our friend Apollos*" (16.12). Paul's directions for

Apollos need not detain us here. We cannot accuse Paul of being so heavenly minded that he was of no earthly use. Good administration is one of the gifts of the Spirit (Romans 12.7).

The object of this book is to "meet Paul", and we shall find much in his letters which is self-revelatory. It is true that he nowhere sits down to write his autobiography. Far from it – he is much more concerned with his Lord and his missionary task than with himself and the details of his own life-story – but occasionally he draws the veil aside. He makes references to episodes such as his controversial meeting with Peter (Galatians 2.11ff.), and remarks about his strictly orthodox Jewish upbringing (Philippians 3.4ff.). Most of the autobiographical references are incidental or illustrate some point he wishes to clarify.

Above all else, his letters present Paul to us as a man infinitely in debt to Christ. His life was a response to the one "who loved me and gave himself up for me" (Galatians 2.20). He could never forget the days when he had persecuted Christ's disciples. Those events left an indelible mark on his personality. As he looked back on the event on the Damascus road, he writes: "it was like a sudden, abnormal birth . . . I am . . . not fit to be called an apostle, because I had persecuted the church of God. However, by God's grace I am what I am" (1 Corinthians 15.8–10). Nor could he forget how Ananias had introduced him to the Christian community at Damascus as "Saul, my brother" (Acts 9.17). There was healing and warmth in the hands which Ananias laid on him, and a world of meaning in the baptism which followed.

"He got up and was baptised" (Acts 9.18). Luke makes no comment in recording that event, but I suspect that there is a strong element of personal recollection in a passage about baptism in Paul's letter to the Romans which he wrote some years afterwards (Romans 8.14ff.). He had indeed been "led by the Spirit of God" that day. As he went down into the water, he died to the old life; he was raised to the new. Never again would he relapse into the old bondage, the "spirit of slavery, leading . . . back into a life of fear". On the contrary, he received at his baptism an endowment of the Spirit which was so powerful that he cried out: "Abba! Father!" He had been adopted into the family. He was enabled to take on his own lips the very word that Jesus had used when he prayed to God. "Abba! Father!" The Spirit of God affirmed within him that he and those members of the Damascus church who had accompanied him to his baptism were "God's children". More than that, they were "heirs of God and fellow-heirs with Christ" (verse 17); sharers of his sufferings now, they would be sharers of his glory hereafter. What wealth! Yes, there is a pronounced autobiographical note in that classic passage.

The letter to the Philippians is the most autobiographical of Paul's letters, and also the happiest. It is full of joy, in spite of the fact that Paul was in prison when he wrote it and was uncertain as to his own future (Philippians 1.19ff.). He might get out, he might remain in prison for a while, or he might be killed. Obviously his readers were hoping and praying for his release. For himself he was strangely carefree. There was much work still awaiting him, and he strongly hoped that nothing would inhibit him from speaking boldly, so that "Christ will display his greatness in me, whether the verdict be life or death" (verse 20). On the other hand, there was his overwhelming conviction that "life is Christ" (verse 21). That unbreakable union of love between him and Christ cannot be ended if the authorities decide to kill him. Indeed, from one point of view, death – the mere destruction of the body – is gain. Departing and being with Christ "is better by far" (verse 23). What a delightful dilemma! He shares it with his readers. They will understand, whichever way Rome decides. He thinks he *will* get out and have the joy of standing by his readers and ensuring their progress and joy in the faith. The uncertainty persists, however (verse 27 begins: "Whatever happens"), so he continues the letter, for his readers' future is sure to be one of conflict and of suffering for Christ.

In fact, there was trouble in Philippi, and Paul, as a good pastor, seeks to deal with it. It is in the course of this work that he writes one of the most self-revelatory passages of all his letters: Philippians 3. The problem was that some members of the church in Philippi insisted that circumcision was essential for all males in the Christian community, as it was required of anyone who considered himself a member of the Jewish community.[3] Paul accuses them of insisting on an external, physical "mutilation" (verse 2). For himself, he puts no confidence in anything external; his pride is in Jesus Christ (verse 3). He cites, in considerable detail, the orthodoxy of his Jewish ancestry and his own conduct and way of life before his conversion. No one could fault him there. But to trust in such things was to trust in externals. God looks on the *heart*. The prophets at their best had insisted on "knowing God" (see, for example, Hosea 4.1, 6; 6.6). Paul speaks, with a wonderful intimacy, of "knowing Christ Jesus my Lord . . . of gaining Christ and finding myself in union with him" (verses 8, 9), with a righteousness derived not from obedience to the dictates of law, however meticulous, but a "righteousness which comes from faith in Christ, given by God in response to faith" (verse 9). This theme recurs, indeed is the main item, in the letter to the Galatians, and is worked out at more leisure in the letter to the Romans. But there is an intimacy in Philippians which has no parallel in Galatians or in Romans. It reaches its climax in the verse where we can hear Paul's heartbeat: "My one desire is to know Christ and the power of his resurrection, and to share his sufferings in growing conformity with his death . . ." (verse 10).

Is this spiritual boasting? Quite the reverse. If one knows the meaning of divine grace, boasting or "human pride", as Paul declares elsewhere, "is excluded" (Romans 3.27). Paul denies having reached perfection. He has not yet taken hold "of that for which Christ once took hold of" him (Philippians 3.12) – memories of the Damascus road again? "I press towards the finishing line," he continues – the word "press" is a strenuous one – "to win the heavenly prize to which God had called" him (verse 14). He relishes the metaphor of the games; he uses it in writing to the Corinthians, whom he urges to "run to win", reminding them that this involves strict training. He alludes to both running and boxing in order to make the point (1 Corinthians 9.24–27).

Paul is not afraid to refer to his own experiences if it will help to clarify his argument. In a self-revelatory passage in the Corinthian correspondence, he tells his readers about the beginning of his visit to them. He had come on to them from Athens (Luke tells the story in Acts 17 and 18). Athens was the intellectual centre of the world, full of pagan temples, philosophers and discussion groups. Paul could make a reference to their own writers and they would recognise the quotations. Corinth was a very different place: pagan temples again, brothels and market-places. Small wonder, then, that Paul came to them "in weakness, in fear, in great trepidation" (1 Corinthians 2.3). Human wisdom or eloquence or argumentation would not avail to break down those citadels of evil. Only the message of a "Christ nailed to the cross" (verse 2), only the power of God himself would ever succeed in establishing what some might think was a contradiction in terms: the church of God at Corinth. (Every good preacher knows the truth of what Paul is saying. He can recollect instances when, having prepared his oration, he is pretty proud of his achievement: the illustrations are fine, the quotations apposite. It's a good piece of work and he is proud of it. Moreover, certain members of the congregation, as they said goodbye at the church door, congratulated him. But in his heart he knows that it was one big flop. He relied on his own cleverness – and that could bring down no citadel of evil. Where in that sermon was the truth about God, the crucified Christ, the power of God himself?)

In no passage of Paul's letters do the words "I" and "me" occur more frequently than in Romans 7, the long introduction to the greatest chapter in the letter, Romans 8. Is his employment of the words simply a rhetorical or literary device? (Such a device is often used: a speaker might say, "It was a terrible experience – I *died* that day." Obviously he did not, for there he is giving the address! But put like that, he makes his point dramatically.) Or is Paul's frequent use of "I" and "me" a straightforward recording of his experience, in a considerable piece of autobiography? Various answers have been given to this question. I believe we have here Paul's unveiling of something that actually happened to him, a sad experience that nevertheless led on to a joyful delivery: "who is there to rescue me from this state of death? Who but God? Thanks be to him through Jesus Christ our Lord!" (Romans 7.24–25).[4]

If this is the case, this chapter is a vivid record of Paul's life before his meeting with Christ, its minor tones giving way to the major ones of Romans 8. He gives us a picture of a torn personality: a young man who knows intellectually what is right, but who is experiencing a tragic inability to put that knowledge into practice. He gives an example: he knew the commandment "You shall not covet" – he had known it from his earliest days. It was an injunction "holy and just and good" (verse 12), and to it he gave his mental assent. But when it came to the crunch, he found himself unable to respond positively: "sin sprang to life and I died" (verse 9). Was there, we wonder, some special incident which had impressed itself on Paul's conscience and to which he here refers? Or was he pin-pointing an oft-repeated failure to obey the command, of which in theory he approved? Specific or general, the experience is universal. Ovid, the Roman poet, gave expression to it in a memorable line: "*Video meliora proboque; deteriora sequor*" – "I see the better and approve it; I follow the worse."

C. H. Dodd, in his commentary on Romans, quotes a famous passage from the *Confessions* of Augustine, whom he describes as "a master of introspective psychology, as well as the greatest interpreter of Paul". Augustine is recalling a youthful prank:

> There was a pear-tree near our vineyard, laden with fruit. One stormy night we rascally youths set out to rob it and carry our spoils away. We took off a huge load of pears – not to feast on them ourselves, but throw them to the pigs – though we ate just enough to have the pleasure of forbidden fruit. They were nice pears, but it was not the pears that my wretched soul coveted, for I had plenty better at home. I picked them simply in order to be a thief. The only feast I got was a feast of iniquity, and that I enjoyed to the full. What was it that I loved in that theft? Was it the pleasure of acting against the law, in order that I, a prisoner under rules, might have a maimed counterfeit of freedom, by doing with impunity what was forbidden, with a dim similitude of omnipotence?[5]

"That is to say that the desire to steal was aroused simply by the prohibition of stealing," Dodd comments. One could cite modern parallels!

". . . my wretched soul" – so Dodd translates Augustine. In Romans 7 "the flesh" is the term that Paul frequently uses. This is the stuff of human nature which we all have in common, with its natural bias to wrong-doing, its openness to evil suggestion. He feels himself "sold as a slave to sin" (verse 14), in sore need of a new master who is powerful enough to rescue him from his bondage. That new master he found in the Christ who revealed himself to Saul on the Damascus road, turned him round in his tracks, apprehended him and apprenticed him, and made it possible for him to shout "Thanks be to God through Jesus Christ our Lord!" (Romans 7.25) and to write that paean of praise which we call Romans 8. The Saul of Romans 7 is the Paul of Romans 8. The writer could never cease to marvel at the grace which had made that transition a fact of experience.

There is another very colourful passage in Paul's letters which I believe to be self-revelatory: 2 Corinthians 12.1–10, but it is best considered in the context of Paul at his prayers, and we shall examine it in the next chapter.

Prayers

I bow my knees before the Father
    From whom every family takes its name.
    May we be strengthened in our inner being
    With power through the Holy Spirit.
    May Christ dwell in our hearts by faith
    As we are being rooted and grounded in love.
    May we know the love of Christ that surpasses
        knowledge
    And be filled with all the fullness of God.[6]

Give us, O God, a sense of
    awe and wonder as we approach you,
    joy at our union with you,
    confidence in your love of us.
When we cannot find words for our prayers,
    remind us of your Spirit
        who takes our groans and interprets them in
            your ears;
        Through Jesus Christ, in whose name we pray.[7]

Teach us, dear Lord, the habit of the upward
    look which seeks for
        help in time of need,
        wisdom in time of doubt.[8]

Give us the grace of gratitude for
    the colour of a sunset,
    the scent of a flower,
    the sound of music,
    the touch of a hand,
    the smile on a face,
    the insight of truth –
    constantly, O blessed Lord.[9]

Grant us, O God, the touch of your Spirit
    which will change our letter-writing from chore
        to ministry.
Then wing our words that they may reach the
    hidden needs of those
    who read them; through Jesus Christ our Lord.[10]

Paul at his Prayers

Abba! Father!

Romans 8.15 and Galatians 4.6

I kneel in prayer to the Father . . .

Ephesians 3.14

I make mention of you in my prayers continually. . . .

Romans 1.9

. . . to him be glory in the church and in Christ Jesus from generation to generation for evermore!

Ephesians 3.21

Prayer is the gateway to theology.

Ecumenical Pilgrims[1]

Paul the *activist?* Yes, intrepid traveller, eager to reach the world for Christ: "I must see Rome" (Acts 19.21) and perhaps Spain? Paul the *controversialist?* Yes, arguing at Athens, rebuking in Galatia, organising at Corinth. Paul the *sufferer?* Yes, beaten with rods, imprisoned, shipwrecked, martyred. But Paul the *man of prayer?* That is not so obvious. We must look carefully at Paul at his prayers.

There are enough prayers strewn across his letters to give us material to work with. That in itself is suggestive. Prayer and letter-writing go hand in hand. Perhaps Paul is setting us an example at this point. Perhaps he is saying: "Letter-writing is a ministry. If, somehow, it can be intertwined with prayer, it can be a powerful ministry." If our hearing apparatus is tuned in carefully, we might overhear him as he prays. "Hush, hush, whisper who dares? Paul the apostle is saying his prayers" – to misquote A. A. Milne.

Prayer was no new thing to Paul when he became a Christian. As a Jewish boy with a devout Jewish background, he came of a praying people. Any nation that can produce the Book of Psalms or the drama of Job has something to teach the world about intercourse with God. But prayer was given a new dimension and a new intimacy when Saul of Tarsus became Paul the apostle. That moment when, at his baptism and entry into the church at Damascus, he came up out of the water and into the resurrection-life, he shouted with his fellow baptisands, "Abba! Father!" Before that, he had watched Stephen in the bloody moments of his martyrdom, and had heard him praying "Lord Jesus, receive my spirit" (Acts 7.59) and at the very moment of death, "Lord, do not hold this sin against them" (Acts 7.60).

There is a delightful phrase in Paul's letters which tells us much about the man himself, about his pastoral care of people and churches, and about the interplay of letter-writing and prayer. Writing to the Romans (Romans 1.9), to the Ephesians and others in his circular letter (Ephesians 1.16), to the

73

Thessalonians (1 Thessalonians 1.2), and to the slave-owner Philemon (Philemon 4), he says that he "*mentions*" them in his prayers. It is as if he paused in his dictation or in his writing, and mentioned one here or a group there, the image of whose faces had just flashed onto the screen of his mind. He paused. It hardly took a moment. Just the mention of a name – sometimes it was literally no more than that. The Holy Spirit, working in the man at prayer, would interpret that name in the heart of the Father. Sometimes the writing stopped for quite a while while Paul held up the one mentioned, into the warmth of the Father's love, but often it was just a mention, no more. It was an arrow prayer. Letters written in that spirit get things done.

Jesus warns us about "babbling on" in our prayers as if the more we pray, the more likely we are to be heard (Matthew 6.7). Sometimes, of course, Paul's prayers are long – we shall consider examples of these later on in this chapter – but often a name, or a few syllables, will say it all: "Abba!"; "Marana tha – Come, Lord!" (1 Corinthians 16.22). And there is a repetition which is *not* "vain", as the Church was soon to learn: "Lord, have mercy; Christ, have mercy; Lord, have mercy," and the Jesus prayer which has blessed so many when they have learned to use it: "Lord Jesus Christ, Son of the living God, have mercy on me, a sinner." It is not the quantity, but the reality that matters.

Paul liked to end his letters with a prayerful greeting: "The grace of our Lord Jesus Christ be with you, my friends." (Galatians 6.18) Or, in its fuller "trinitarian" form: "The grace of the Lord Jesus Christ, and the love of God, and the fellowship of the Holy Spirit, be with you all." (2 Corinthians 13.14) There is enough in that short prayer to feed the soul and enrich the spirit for a long time. Consider the ordering of the clauses. "The grace of the Lord Jesus" comes first. This reflects the order of Paul's experience. Saul had prayed as a boy and as a young man, and those prayers had surely been accepted, but when God had put him on his back and made him look up (his old pride shattered, his emptiness all he had to offer), it was the overwhelming *grace* of the Lord Jesus that broke him and remade him. He could never be the same again. Through the grace of his Lord Jesus Christ he saw into the heart of God, and it was all love – love for him in his plight, love for the world in its need, love to the uttermost. Grace, love and fellowship – that bond which had united the original band of disciples, so different from one another socially and politically, into a body which cohered, which held together in spite of the strains. That fellowship was the nucleus of the Christian Church.

If we wanted to find three words to sum up not only the experience of Paul but the essence of his message to the world, we could not do better than grace, love and fellowship, the key words of what has become the second-best-known prayer of the Christian Church: "The grace of the Lord Jesus Christ, and the love of God, and the fellowship of the Holy Spirit, be with you all."

Then there are what might be called "the outburst prayers" of Paul. Among them we should, I suppose, include those utterances when Paul found himself "speaking in tongues". It was a gift of the Spirit which Paul valued: "I am more gifted in tongues than any of you," he wrote to the Corinthians (1 Corinthians 14.18). His heart was so full that words failed him and God took over. We cannot overhear such prayers. It was holy ground to Paul, and we must needs stand aside.

However, there are in his writings passages where exposition gives way to thanksgiving, where doctrine runs into doxology. Sometimes it is little more than an ascription of glory to God which he slips into an argument, almost interrupting the course of the discussion. For example, while he is dealing sternly with the matter of people who misuse their bodies in sexual activity, the mention of the Creator God causes him to exclaim, "Blessed is he for ever, Amen" (Romans 1.25). Similarly, in Romans 9.1–5 he is writing of his intense desire that his Jewish friends, so richly endowed with spiritual wealth,

75

should enter into their inheritance in Christ. From them he lifts his eyes to God: "May God, supreme above all, be blessed for ever! Amen." A better and longer instance of teaching running into praise occurs at the end of a long argumentative passage in the letter to the Romans which takes up three chapters (9 to 11). Paul has been wrestling with the mystery of God's dealings with humankind. The argument ends. Words and logic fail him. He can only worship in a series of exclamations and questions and ascription:

> How deep are the wealth and the wisdom and the knowledge of God! How inscrutable his judgements, how unsearchable his ways! "Who knows the mind of the Lord? Who has been his counsellor?" "Who has made a gift to him first, and earned a gift in return?" From him and through him and for him all things exist – to him be glory for ever! Amen. (Romans 11.33–6)

The circular letter which we call the letter to the Ephesians divides naturally into two parts: the first three chapters are doctrinal in content, dealing with such matters as the glory of Christ in the church, God's grace to Gentiles and Paul's prayer for his readers. The last three chapters are mainly ethical, dealing with Christian conduct and Christian relationships in the light of God's action in Christ. The doctrinal section ends with a great outburst of doxology: "Now to him who is able through the power that is at work among us to do immeasurably more than all we can ask or conceive, to him be glory in the church and in Christ Jesus from generation to generation for evermore! Amen." (Ephesians 3.20–21) The words are full of amazement and adoration. The ethical section ends on a more reserved note, with a greeting which is essentially a prayer: "Peace to the community and love with faith, from God the Father and the Lord Jesus Christ. God's grace be with all who love our Lord Jesus Christ with undying love." (Ephesians 6.23–4)

The attitude of Paul at his prayers is one of quiet confidence in his God. There is no wheedling here, no currying favour, no attempt to bend God's arm. Rather, there is behind these prayers a holy boldness. In Christ, Paul says, "we have freedom of access to God, with the confidence born of trust in him". The Greek word translated as "freedom" is used in the context of prayer and worship by the unknown writer of the letter to the Hebrews (4.16 and 10.19). It means joyful, bold confidence, basically "saying everything". There is nothing to hide, nor is there anything too small to mention. There is a way open into the Presence, and the Presence is love.

If there is no wheedling, neither is there any cockiness. The familiarity of a hand-shaking relationship with God is wholly foreign to Paul, and indeed to all the writers of the New Testament. Awe and wonder – that is the atmosphere in which Paul prays. We have been given "access to that grace in which we now live" (Romans 5.2), and that access is enjoyed in a relationship with God which is entered into in prayer. Confidence and reverence must mark the approach of a man to his God, a woman to her Creator.

To leave the matter there, however, would be to over-simplify the human situation. That very chapter (Romans 8) which speaks of the Christian as a child crying out in joy and wonder "Abba! Father!" (verse 15) is one that wrestles with the fact of a universe which has gone wrong. It is a universe "waiting" (verse 19), "subject to frustration" (verse 20), bound with "the shackles of mortality" (verse 21), groaning "as if in the pangs of childbirth" (verse 22). Nor is the Church exempt from that sentence of mortality. These people, to whom the Spirit has been given, these firstfruits of a future harvest, these are the expectant people, the not-yet people, the hope-full people. They crane their necks; they know how to endure and never give in. Meanwhile they are the praying people, but they are not very good at it – they do not even know how they ought to pray, or what they ought to pray for. There is a realistic touch to Paul's writing here with which we can all sympathise. Which of us cannot remember a time (maybe many times) when we too have felt lost and unable to pray. There is a whisper in our ear: "Better give up praying – it doesn't make sense." Paul will have none of this temptation. To give in to it would be to deny the presence of God's Spirit, ready as he is to "come to the aid of our weakness". All we can manage is a groan; how can we know that we have rightly assessed the need of the person we are praying for, or, for that matter, our own need? Don't worry, the apostle reassures us. The Spirit will take that groan and interpret it in the Father's ear. He will understand what the Spirit means and will co-operate with those who love him, for in the mind of God is a plan determined before we were born. He intends us to "share the likeness of his Son" (Romans 8.29). The sculpting process will be life-long, but the Master-sculptor, having once set himself to the task, will never abandon it.

I note that Paul writes in the plural: "We do not even know . . . the Spirit himself is pleading for us" (Romans 8.26). Here again is encouragement for the person at prayer. His solo prayer is a poor thing, but he does not pray alone. He is one small part of the great praying Church. The stream of that Church's prayer has been flowing throughout the ages. It is going on today and will continue to the great consummation. Paul slips his little prayer into that stream. To change the metaphor: the praying Church is a vast orchestra; I am not much good with my little lone fiddle, but I go on playing – and praying – in the great symphony.

In one sense, it does not matter very much if we get the wording wrong. We are limited in our understanding of our own needs and of the needs of others. Sometimes we can do little more than stutter when we try to verbalise our prayers. God understands. Indeed, he can take a prayer the granting of which would be to our loss, the denial of which would lead to our greater good. There is an excellent example of this in 2 Corinthians 12.1–10.

It is a strange passage. We spiritual midgets do not always

understand the ways of the giants. I think Paul is inviting us to share with him an instance when God dealt with him with a special intimacy. For reasons best known to himself, Paul will not say "I". He, as it were, stands outside himself in a state of ecstasy and seeks to see, and to relate to his correspondents, a great spiritual experience that happened to him. "I know a Christian man who fourteen years ago ... was caught up as far as the third heaven." (2 Corinthians 12.2) Of course he knows; he *was* that man! "Caught up"? It was his way of saying: "I had a great spiritual experience. I heard words so secret that human words may not repeat them." It was a revelation, a divine revelation. Such experiences carry with them their own temptations, and Paul was aware of this. They could lead to the folly of boasting about them – human flesh is frail – so God acted to keep his servant's feet firmly on the earth. Paul was given a thorn in his flesh, a *skolops* (verse 7).

This is an ugly word for an ugly thing. Precisely what it was Paul does not say. The word can mean a stake, a stick with a point at its top. It can mean a fish-hook – and any fishing enthusiast who has got that in his finger instead of in the fish's mouth will know the feeling! Was it in Paul's case recurrent malaria or some such unpleasant nuisance? Quite probably. We do not know. "Three times I begged the Lord to rid me of it," he tells us (verse 8). Of course, God is the God of health and desires the well-being of his children. "Three times" – Paul made quite sure that God was listening! Of course he was. He answered, and the answer was "no". "No, Paul; I will show you a better way, and teach you the deeper meaning of 'my grace'." "My grace is all you need; power is most fully seen in weakness." (verse 9)

It is a difficult lesson to learn – not "out of", but "in"; not "on the dry land" but "through the waters":

> When you pass through water I shall be with you;
> when you pass through rivers they will not
>   overwhelm you;

79

walk through fire and you will not be scorched,
through flames, and they will not burn you.
I am the Lord your God . . .

(Isaiah 43.2–3)

The passage ends with the picture of a contented man – and
here Paul does write in the first person: "So I am content with
a life of weakness, insult, hardship, persecution, and distress,
all for Christ's sake; for when I am weak, then I am strong."
(2 Corinthians 12.10) At his prayers, Paul had learnt his
lesson.

At the beginning of this chapter, I wrote of the possibility of
"overhearing Paul as he prays". In two great prayers in
Ephesians (1.15–23 and 3.14–21) we can overhear him, perhaps
better than anywhere else, as he prays for what C. S. Lewis
calls "our great, permanent, objective necessities". There is
nothing petty in these prayers. The horizon is wide, the scope
unlimited. Paul's mind reaches out to "the heavenly realms"
(Ephesians 1.3) and embraces "the universe, everything in
heaven and on earth" (verse 10), one day to be brought into a
unity in Christ. We shall examine these prayers in some detail,
a task which may spur some readers to do likewise with Paul's
other prayers.

Ephesians 1.15–23[2]

The prayer is closely packed. Phrase is piled on phrase. We
may best approach it by asking two questions: first, to whom
does Paul pray? Second, what does he pray?

To whom does he pray? The answer is, first, to "the God of our
Lord Jesus Christ" (verse 17) – a somewhat mysterious phrase.
What does "of" mean? It must mean the God to whom Jesus
prayed. His God is our God. The God to whom he prayed in
the intimacy of an unbroken communion is the same God to

whom we come, however falteringly and with however dim a vision. But "the God of our Lord Jesus Christ" means more than this. It means the God whom Jesus disclosed, the God of whom he spoke in terms of kingship and fatherhood. In praying to him, then, we must never think unworthily, never allow a thought of him which is incompatible with the teaching of Jesus to enter our mind.

Second, Paul prays to "the Father of [the] glory" (verse 17) – a phrase unique in the New Testament ("the all-glorious Father" is a paraphrase). It is just conceivable that "the glory" may be a reference to Christ himself, in which case "the Father of the Glory" would be an elaboration of the first phrase, "the God of our Lord Jesus Christ". But it is much more probable that the phrase points to the majesty of the God to whom those who pray can only come with awe.

What does Paul pray? He prays that God "may confer on you the spiritual gifts of wisdom and vision, with the knowledge of him that they bring" (verse 17). A more literal translation would be: "a spirit of wisdom and unveiling in an experiential knowledge of him". Paul knew the literature which had grown up round the concept of wisdom, of which the Book of Proverbs and the Book of Wisdom (or the Wisdom of Solomon) are best known. The writer of Wisdom had written in a prayer somewhat similar to Paul's: "Send her forth from your holy heaven . . . so that she may labour at my side and I may learn what is pleasing to you" (Wisdom 9.10).

The word "vision" or "unveiling" is explained in Ephesians 1.18: "your inward eyes . . . enlightened". It signifies the drawing aside of an obscuring curtain: "Draw from our timid eyes the veil." Most of us go through life with our eyes half shut, blind to "the many-splendoured thing". The sights and sounds around us combine to cast a veil over our eyes and so we miss the knowledge of God. When Paul prays that the inward eyes of his readers may be enlightened, the words he uses mean literally "the eyes of your heart". The heart being the seat of affection and will, vision must lead to action, illumination to decision.

"... the knowledge of him" (verse 17) – this is knowledge with a difference. The usual Greek word for knowledge is *gnosis*, but here (and often elsewhere) Paul adds a prefix, making the word *epignosis*. It is as if he tells us, by the very form of the word which he uses: "Intellectual knowledge by itself is not enough. The Greeks tried the way of the intellect, but to them the cross was only folly. More than intellect is called for. Knowledge must be brought into the sphere of spiritual experience." Knowledge by itself all too easily "breeds conceit; it is love that builds" (see 1 Corinthians 8.1–3). "That I may know him" – this is the experiential knowledge of Christ which is life indeed.

That prayer being granted, three things will follow:

1 Paul's readers will know what is the hope to which God calls them. We have seen that for Paul "hope" is no vague word. For him, it is the confidence that the image of God in which humankind was made will be restored after its defacement by sin: "... we exult in the hope of the divine glory that is to be ours" (Romans 5.2).

2 They will know "how rich and glorious is the share he offers you among his people in their inheritance" (verse 18). In Ephesians 2 and 3 Paul makes much of the fact that Gentiles share with Jews in the redemption which God has made known in Christ. It is great to be in the family of God, with a rich Father at its head. The translation is a free one; literally, Paul writes: "what is the wealth of the glory of his inheritance in the holy ones". Can this mean that *God* has an inheritance, consisting of the saints, "the blessed company of all faithful people"? (Israel in the Old Testament is referred to as "God's glory", for example in Psalm 78.61 ("glory" is translated as "pride" in the *Revised English Bible*).

Another Psalmist (149.4, BCP) speaks of God "taking pleasure in his people".) Is Paul here exulting in the thought of God's wealth in the Church which he had bought at the price of the blood of his Son?

3 They will know "how vast are the resources of his power open to us who have faith" (Ephesians 1.19). In Old Testament days God's power had been signally manifested, the strength of his arm shown, in the rescue of his people from the tyranny of the Egyptians. Now the greatness of his power is to be seen in the resurrection of Jesus. That power is available to those "who have faith", those who trust in him. Penniless, they own the world! (2 Corinthians 6.10)

Here, at verse 19, strictly speaking the prayer ends. It becomes an elaboration of the point Paul has just made about the power of God as seen in Christ's resurrection and ascension-enthronement. The language of verse 21 is probably coloured by the language of those Gnostic sects whose members envisaged a kind of ladder of intermediary powers between human beings and their material world on the one hand and God on the other. Paul uses their terms for his own purpose, to state that, whatever powers we like to think of in the universe, above them all towers the figure of Christ risen and enthroned, head of "the church which is his body, the fullness of him who is filling the universe in all its parts" (verses 22–23).

Ephesians 3.14–21

We shall ask here the same two questions which we asked about the first prayer in this letter: to whom does Paul pray, and what does he pray? First let us look at the structure of the chapter.

Paul begins the prayer: "With this in mind I pray for you, I, Paul who for the sake of you Gentiles am now the prisoner of Christ Jesus –" (verse 1). He is going to say "I kneel in prayer to the Father" (see verse 14), but the mention of "you Gentiles" temporarily distracts him. He goes off at a tangent, and it is some time before he picks up his prayer again. It is a splendid digression, a meditation which serves as a useful background for the prayer and helps us to understand it.

Paul says that he has received a revelation: "It was by a revelation that [God's] secret purpose was made known to me." (verse 3) What was this secret, not disclosed to mankind? It was that through the gospel a new race has been created, a race in which the old terminology of Jew and Gentile, hitherto so terribly divisive, so productive of ideas of racial superiority, counts no more. The Church has been born. The fellowship has been created.

Paul marvels at "the unfathomable riches of Christ" (verse 8) and at "the wisdom of God in its infinite variety" (verse 10). This conjures up the image of a jewel, flashing different hues as it is turned to different lights. He marvels, too, at the miracle of grace by which this disclosure has been made to him of all people, calling himself "less than the least of all God's people" (verse 8). It would be wrong to dismiss this phrase as mock humility. Paul could never forget Stephen's death and his own persecution of members of the early Church. If, as I believe, he uses the phrase with humble objectivity, it is a mark of his own growth in holiness – the nearer a person draws to God, the more conscious does he become of his own littleness.

Against that rich digressive background, Paul picks up in verse 14 the prayer he began in verse 1: "With this in mind then, I kneel in prayer". Often the Jews stood to pray. The fact that he is kneeling may underline the urgency with which Paul prays and indicate the awe he feels in coming into the Presence of God.

To whom does he pray? The answer is, to the Father. As Jesus had prayed and as he had taught his disciples to pray, so Paul prays. The title is elaborated, however. God is "the Father, from whom every family in heaven and on earth takes its name" (verses 14–15). The families "in heaven" are presumably the angels. The families "on earth" are those known to Paul, the little groups in Asia Minor and elsewhere. Often weak, always in a minority, sometimes persecuted, they were nevertheless all families of the one great Father whose grace is available to all. This is the God to whom prayer is addressed.

What does Paul pray? For his readers to be given "inward strength and power" (verse 16). How will this happen? Apart from the doxology in verses 20–21, practically all of the rest of the prayer is devoted to answering that question.

Paul tells his readers that strength will come, not by human effort, but through God's Spirit (verse 16). A plant does not grow by striving but by being open to the resources of nature which are available to it. This is what John meant by "dwelling in Christ, as the branch dwells in the vine" (John 15.1–7). Of course, Christians must watch and pray; they must have discipline and self-denial. But "inward strength and power" are primarily the work of the Spirit. *His* fruit is love, joy, peace.

Paul puts this in another way when he speaks of Christ dwelling "in your hearts in love" (verse 17). This is the nearest phrase in Paul's vocabulary to that dwelling in Christ described by John: his mind, our mind; his will, our will; his peace, our peace; his joy, our joy. This is the intimacy, the strength of union with Christ. (Incidentally, do these words "in love" go with the preceding or the following words? The Greek will bear either. *The Revised English Bible* goes for the former, other versions for the latter. What do you think?)

"With deep roots and firm foundations" (verse 17): agriculture and architecture in a forceful mixture of metaphors! It occurs again in Colossians 2.7: "Be rooted in him, be built in him ...". As roots go down and foundations become ever firmer, Paul's readers will get to know Christ's love, which is "beyond knowledge" (verse 19). To know the unknowable, to grasp the ungraspable – language breaks down under the immensity of the concept with which the writer is dealing. His readers will understand.

We have omitted one phrase: "in company with all God's people" (verse 18). Paul declares that knowledge of the love of Christ which is beyond knowledge does not come in self-imposed isolation, but in company with all God's people. "Christian doctrine knows nothing of an atomistic individualism" – John Whale was right.[3] "We possess the mind of Christ" – we, not I (1 Corinthians 2.16). We dare not cut ourselves off from the illumination which comes to us from other Christians – women and men whose backgrounds, nationalities and cultures differ from our own – nor from other branches of Christ's holy, catholic Church. Hence the urgency of the ecumenical movement.

This, then, is a prayer for "inward strength and power". It ends with a doxology to the Lord of power: "to him who is able through the power which is at work among us to do immeasurably more than all we can ask or conceive" (verse 20). This doxology is what Emerson calls "a sally of love and admiration".[4] It is an attempt to express the profound truth of the power of Christ available to all, through faith, by his Spirit, in the Church. This is the source of both Paul's Christian character and his missionary activity.

It is – to appropriate some words at the end of Pope John XXIII's *Diary of a Soul* – "the humble prayer of a Christian, who thinks of sin but is aware of forgiveness, thinks of death but with a heart that is sure of resurrection, knows the magnitude of his own unworthiness but knows even better the greater magnitude of the Lord's mercy".[5]

"To him be glory in the Church and in Christ Jesus from generation to generation for evermore! Amen." (Ephesians 3.21)

Prayers

I make mention of you in my prayers continually . . . .

Romans 1.9

Abba! Father!

Romans 8.15 and Galatians 4.6

The grace of the Lord Jesus Christ
and the love of God,
and the fellowship of the Holy Spirit,
be with you all.

2 Corinthians 13.14

. . . through our inarticulate groans the Spirit himself is pleading for us, and God who searches our inmost being knows
what the Spirit means . . . .

Romans 8.26–27

How deep are the wealth
and the wisdom and the knowledge of God!
How inscrutable his judgements,
how unsearchable his ways! . . .
From him and through him and for him all things exist –
to him be glory for ever! Amen.

Romans 11.33, 36

Now to him who is able through the power which is at work
among us to do immeasurably more than all we can ask or
conceive, to him be glory in the church and in Christ Jesus
from generation to generation for evermore! Amen.

Ephesians 3.20–21

87

A Man in Christ

For in him [Christ] God in all his fullness chose to dwell . . . .

Colossians 1.19

———

. . . knowledge of the glory of God in the face of Jesus Christ.

2 Corinthians 4.6

———

For anyone united to Christ, there is a new creation . . . .

2 Corinthians 5.17

———

It is through faith that you are all sons of God in union with Christ Jesus.

Galatians 3.26

———

My one desire is to know Christ and the power of his resurrection, and to share his sufferings . . . .

Philippians 3.10

———

I press towards the finishing line, to win the heavenly prize to which God has called me in Christ Jesus.

Philippians 3.14

Few men who have left a significant mark on the pages of history – and without doubt Paul was one such – have been more misjudged than the Paul whom we are seeking to meet in this book. Ask even the average churchgoer who hears his letters read in church services, and maybe reads them sometimes at home, whether they think he was a friendly man, and I guarantee you will get a very dubious answer. "Warm-hearted? Loving? Outgoing?" Many of those questioned, if they were answering honestly, would say "No". When they try to picture Paul, they probably see a face that is stern, if not forbidding, chilly if not cold; a learned man, yes, but academic to the point of being pernickety.

I believe that such a negative reply would indicate a grave misunderstanding of Paul, for reasons that anyone who has read this book as far as this will have deduced. However, the point is worth pursuing, indeed must be pursued.

We have seen that Paul, contrary to his usual plan, spent three years at Ephesus. That is a long time. He had very close dealings with the Christians there. The time came when he knew that he must leave Ephesus and make for Jerusalem. He summoned the leaders of the church at Ephesus to meet him at the port before he embarked. What was the atmosphere at that meeting? Was the elders' attitude "Good riddance. Glad to see the back of him"? Not at all. Let his travel companion, Luke, describe the scene: "he knelt down with them and prayed. There were loud cries of sorrow from them all, as they folded Paul in their arms and kissed him; what distressed them most was his saying that they would never see his face again." (Acts 20.36–8) And how did Paul and Luke regard the parting? Luke puts it bleakly: "We tore ourselves away from them" (Acts 21.1). No comment is needed.

One of the least-read passages in Paul's letters is the last chapter of Romans. The first part of this chapter consists of a list of names, and the reader might well pray that he is never called upon to read it in public, for there are some tongue-

twisters in it! But look at it more closely and it is full of interest. It begins with Paul's commending of Phoebe, a woman
whom he describes as "a fellow-Christian who is a minister
in the church at Cenchreae" (Romans 16.1). There are many
women in the list, one of whom, Junia, is "eminent among the
apostles" (verse 7) (that is if Junia, not Junias, is the right reading; note also Julia, or Julian, in verse 15). Rufus' mother is
mentioned in verse 13, "whom I call mother too" – a delightful
touch. I imagine that Paul had a good many "mothers" in the
places of his travels who would give him a meal and a bed
and a welcome and make up for that home of his own which
he had given up for Christ's sake. The recurrence of the word
"dear" indicates the nature of his relationship with people
about whom we know nothing but whom he knew well. Some
had "risked their necks to save his life" (verse 4); some had
been "comrades in captivity" with him (verse 7); Gaius is
described as Paul's "host and host of the whole congregation"
(verse 23). In verse 16 the Christians are bidden to "greet one
another with the kiss of peace", a phrase found in three other
passages in Paul's letters. (Is there a hint of liturgical direction
here, or is it the Pauline equivalent of a big hug?)

Mull over this chapter and the greetings which Paul sends in
others of his letters, and we see a man to whom friendship
with others of very mixed backgrounds and outlooks meant
much – a friendly man, at the very least.

But we must go further than that, if we are to understand
the man. ". . . through the Holy Spirit he has given us, God's
love has flooded our hearts," Paul wrote to the Romans (5.5).
This is more than a generalisation. It has behind it his own
personal experience – it is autobiographical. A favourite Whit-
sun hymn asks the Holy Spirit to "bend the stubborn heart
and will; melt the frozen, warm the chill; guide the steps that
go astray". The spirit of that prayer was very positively
answered in the case of Paul.

In Chapter 5, we noticed Paul's fondness, when writing

about his prayers, of "mentioning" people before God (p. 74). He had ample opportunity to do this as he tramped mile after weary mile; as he sailed the Mediterranean (for his times at sea were not *all* shipwreck!); as he lay in prison; when he could not sleep.[1] What sort of recollections did he have? He could not waste these long hours, letting his mind wander uselessly. He must occupy at least some of the time in the ministry of "mentioning". Is Romans 16 a list of people for whom he prayed constantly, regularly? I think it may well be.

As his mind – and his prayers – ranged out over these individuals, scattered in little groups across the world he knew, he must have felt very much linked to them all. Most of them were insignificant, as the world judges significance. Often the groups were small. But the individuals and groups were all part of the Church, a living entity which he described variously as the body of Christ, the building of which Christ is the corner-stone, the bride of Christ. He was one with them in Christ. They were one with him in Christ. There is a unity here which transcends the limits of space and time.

"In Christ": the phrase occurs again and again in Paul's writings. "If anyone be in Christ, there is a new creation" (2 Corinthians 5.17). "I know a man in Christ" (2 Corinthians 12.2; "a Christian man" (REB) is not a literal translation). "No condemnation for those in Christ Jesus" (Romans 8.1). We could extend the list.

The phrase has become familiar to us because of the frequency of its occurrence. It trips off our tongues without our giving it much thought. But it is a strange expression. How can a man or woman be a person "in" somebody else? How can a group be "in" Christ Jesus? Yet those two words dominate Paul's thinking and quite obviously go to the roots of his experience and of his conduct as a member of Christ's body.

We had best seek an answer to our question by way of some analogies. None is complete in itself, and all are limited by the fact that they *are* analogies, but it may be hoped that, taken

91

together, they point towards an insight into what was basic in Paul's experience as a Christian man.

Here is a cutting which the gardener hopes will one day be a healthy plant. An incision is made into the parent tree. The frail little cutting is grafted into it, so that the two become one living unit. In it is its one hope of life. Without it, it will die.

Here is a person enjoying a meal. He swallows something which "goes the wrong way". There is an obstruction to the inflow of air. But air is essential to his life as a human being. It is the element in which he lives. Without it he will die.

Here is a fish, happy in the river or the sea. But land that fish on the bank and leave him there, and there will be a few frantic jerks and he will die. Water is his element. In it is his life. Without it he will die.

Here is a young woman. She has grown; she has graduated; she has got her job. She loves that job – "I would not be any-where else in the world," she says. "She is in her element," we say. Put her in any other sphere, and she will wilt.

Here is Vladimir Ashkenazy. I listened to him playing the soloist's part as André Previn conducted the Royal Philharmonic Orchestra in a performance of Beethoven's Fourth Piano Concerto. I watched Ashkenazy almost with awe. As I did so, I saw a man who – is this putting it too strongly? – was in communion with Beethoven. No doubt for decades he had studied and practised the scores of his works. But there was more to the performance than the mere production of the notes which Beethoven had put down on paper. It seemed that the spirit of the master had entered into and got hold of the disciple. Ashkenazy was wholly Beethoven's man; in a manner of speaking, he had become one with him. The unity of author and performer was so close that Ashkenazy might almost have said: "It is not I who play. Beethoven plays in me." Nor did that unity diminish the personality of Ashkenazy. It heightened it. He came into his own when his gifts were at Beethoven's disposal.[2]

Paul was "a man in Christ". He was in love with his Lord, totally satisfied to be laid hold of by Christ and to become an apprentice of his. His heart had been flooded by God's love. He was in his element, a man fulfilled. Death had no dominion over him. "To depart" was to be "with Christ" (Philippians 1.23). "In Christ" here leads on to "with Christ" there. Neither life nor death could separate him from the love of God in Christ Jesus his Lord.

One of the most remarkable Christians of this century was Alexander Men (1935–90). Too little known to most people outside the USSR, he was an outstanding leader of the Church there during some of its most difficult days and in the early years after Gorbachev's accession to power in 1985. That event brought no immediate relief to the Church. Indeed, in 1986 Men was publicly denounced for the stand that he had taken with such fearlessness in the cause of Christ and his Church. In 1988, however, Christianity was officially acknowledged as a legitimate and valued part of the Russian heritage. *Perestroika* had arrived. The windows had been opened and fresh breezes began to blow. The work to which Men had devoted himself for many years (he was ordained in 1960) – teaching, writing, baptising, building up the Church – could now be carried on in the open, and Men applied himself to the task with an urgency which might have been taken as a sign that he suspected his time to be short. The "anti-libertarians" were at work, however, and shortly after the celebrations of Men's 30 years as a priest, they got him: on his way back from giving a lecture in Moscow two of them struck him on the head with an axe and killed him. So died a man of superb devotion and intellect, a pastor with a great love for his people, one of the greatest martyrs of a century which has produced a singularly long list of Christians faithful unto death.

I mention him here because he had entered deeply into what it meant – to him personally, and to his people – to be "in Christ". I quote from a lecture which he gave on the night before he was murdered, a lecture in which "Fr. Alexander reiterates his note of optimism: that the victory has already been won, the new life has come and Christianity is only in its infancy, only at the beginning":[3]

> Eternal love bound [Paul] to Christ so that it seemed to him that he bore on himself the wounds of Christ, that he died with him on the cross and was resurrected with him. He said: "I no longer live, but Christ lives in me. Together with him I died, and together with him I have risen to life." (Galatians 2.20)[4]

Later in the lecture, Men said:

> When his disciples felt he was leaving them, [Jesus] spoke some prophetic and eternal words: "I do not leave you orphaned but I will come back to you", and this continues and is happening today. All the deepest Christian experience is founded only on this; all the rest, as it were, are superficial layers.[5]

Men asks: "What does it mean, to be saved?" He answers: "It means uniting one's ephemeral temporal life with the immortal, with God – that's what salvation is." Again he asks: "What does faith in Jesus Christ mean?" He answers first by asking another question: "Faith in the fact that this man lived on earth? That is not faith but knowledge. Belief in the fact that he came from other worlds? That's also true, but it's just theory." He points back to "the faith that was announced in the Old Testament . . . when Abraham said 'Yes' to God, or more correctly, didn't say anything, but quietly obeyed God's call, that was when faith was born." To the Christian, "Jesus Christ is the human face of the infinite, the ineffable, the inscrutable, the unbounded, the nameless." To be "in Christ", quietly to obey God's call, is to be "saved". Men declares:

> Between the Creator and the created lies an abyss, like the abyss between the absolute and the contingent: we can

never leap over, neither logically nor existentially. Yet there is a bridge thrown over this abyss, and Paul experienced this bridge himself because he saw Christ and was inwardly united to him.[6]

Salvation, faith and grace (see above pp. 35ff.): these major concepts in Paul's experience and writings come together in the phrase "in Christ". That union binds together the people of God and is commemorated and renewed when "the blessed company of all faithful people" meet for the eucharistic feast.

We pursue our exploration into the meaning of the phrase "in Christ", and more particularly into what it meant to Paul to be "a man in Christ". We shall not "meet Paul", in any real sense, until we have dug deep into this concept. In the first part of 2 Corinthians 4, the apostle tries to put his finger on what is at the heart of the ministry which God has given him and what it is that enables him never to lose heart and become the victim of despair (verses 1 and 16). The core of the message he proclaims is "the good news of the glory of Christ", whom he describes as "the image of God" (verse 4). Jesus is similarly described in Colossians 1.15 as "the image of the invisible God" – the *icon* of God, or "the human face of the infinite", as Alexander Men puts it. Robert Bridges' translation of the Greek hymn, which goes back at least to the fourth century, captures Paul's thought:

> O gladsome light, O grace
> Of God the Father's face,
> The eternal splendour wearing;
> Celestial, holy, blest,
> Our Saviour Jesus Christ,
> Joyful in your appearing.[7]

Paul spurns the very idea that he himself might be at the heart of what he proclaims – perish the thought! "It is not ourselves that we proclaim; we proclaim Christ Jesus as Lord, and

ourselves as your servants for Jesus' sake." (2 Corinthians 4.5)
He searches for an illustration of that new dawn which has
brought him light. He finds it in the creation story as given in
Genesis 1. "For the God who said, 'Out of darkness light shall
shine,' has caused his light to shine in our hearts, the light
which is knowledge of the glory of God in the face of Jesus
Christ." (verse 6) "In the beginning . . . darkness covered the
deep . . ." (Genesis 1.1, 2). God spoke, and there was light. In
the beginning chaos reigned. God spoke, and there was order.
Darkness and chaos – how well those words describe Paul's own
condition before the light shone on the Damascus road and
blinded him with its glory! And how well those words describe
the lives of many in Corinth who had been brought out from
the darkness of perplexity, of heathenism and dissipation, into
the glorious liberty of the children of God. "The light which
is knowledge of the glory of God" is found "in the face of Jesus
Christ" (2 Corinthians 4.6). That face had looked down on the
recumbent figure of Saul of Tarsus, in infinite compassion and
love. How could he say "No"? "Bliss was it in that dawn to be
alive".[7] "In Christ" Paul was in his element.

To be "in Christ" is to be in "the Body of Christ". The
phrase is as corporate as it is individual; one cannot be "in
Christ" and at the same time be divorced from his Body. Also:
"Christ is not Christ without the community of love which
he founded" (J. H. Oldham).[8] The Head of the Church, risen
and victorious, sends life coursing out from himself to all the
members of his body. He binds them together. The ascended
Christ gives gifts to his Church in rich profusion, so that his
Body may go into the world as a missionary community, and
as a *united* Body. The very idea of separate "churches", as we
speak of them today, "would have been a jar to the apostles
and evangelists," writes Franklin C. Fry. "'Is Christ divided?'
was an absurdity to the mind of St Paul. The dividedness of
the church does violence to the Holy Ghost who lives in it."[9]

This essential corporateness is at the heart of Paul's vehemence when he sees heresy attacking the members of the Body. People get annoyed with Paul because, as they would say, he keeps "banging on" against those whom he would charge with heretical teaching. Such people could point to passages where he uses very sharp language in describing them: "You stupid Galatians!" (Galatians 3.1), "those dogs" (Philippians 3.2), and so on. Was such language due to a lack of love on the part of the apostle? Or could it be compared to the surgeon's use of a knife when he sees that his patient's life is at risk? Paul knew and loved his readers with a deeply caring concern. There were occasions when it would have been cruel to be mealy-mouthed. In the sphere of religious controversy today, the language we use is different from that used in the controversies of the early centuries of the Church's history, and that, no doubt, is all to the good. We do not call those who hold views opposite to our own "stupid". We (rightly) enter into dialogue with them. What we must *not* do is to give the impression that truth does not matter. It does. Truth is sacred, and of that truth we are trustees. Belief is the motive power behind action.

Discernment, the guidance of the Spirit, is called for. Paul knew where to fight his battles – what was worth fighting for, where to spend his energies. Let me illustrate.

Galatians and Romans

Of the letters to the Galatians and to the Romans, Galatians is the earlier. From one point of view, it is the rough model of which Romans is the finished statue. The main issue with which both letters deal is essentially the same. There are indications that Galatians was written – one might almost say "dashed off" – to meet an immediate need. There is no polish to the letter. It is not always easy to follow, and there is one passage (Galatians 4.21ff.) in which Paul's method of argument reminds us of his rabbinic background and which has caused the commentators many sleepless nights! Romans shows signs of more leisurely thought and of careful planning; it is magisterial in its onward march. The heat of Galatians is lacking in Romans, although the urgency remains the same. Let us examine the issue through Paul's eyes.

A few decades ago an event had occurred in a corner of the Roman empire: a baby was born. After a brief life, a crucifixion took place, followed by a resurrection – and an ascension – and a gift of the Spirit which fell on the followers of the One at the heart of these events. All this (we will call it, for short, "the Christ-event") was a disclosure of the nature and activity of God. While being prepared for long ago, it was in its fulfilment unique. This revelation of a truth previously undisclosed was of cosmic proportions. God's clock had struck at God's moment in history. Now a world was waiting to hear and, maybe, to respond to the divine message carried within the Christ-event. Mission – the passing on of the news of this event – was of the essence of the Body of believers. Did the message embrace all humankind? Was it universal? Clearly, it was a manifestation of the immensity of God's love for the world. Was that love unconditional?

There were those in Jerusalem, where the Christ-event had been centred, who took it for granted that all male Christians should be circumcised; after all, Jesus had been a Jew and they themselves were Jews. But, very early on, the appeal of the Christian message was such that non-Jews were being drawn to obedience to the magnetic Christ (the high official of the Queen of Ethiopia was a case in point – see Acts 8.26ff.). Many non-Jewish people "listened-in" to the Jews as they worshipped in their synagogues, and were drawn to much of what Judaism stood for. Was it to be demanded of them that all their males should be circumcised if they were to be followers of "The Way"? In short, was the Christian community to be a kind of sub-section of Judaism? Was the door of entry to the Church

98

to be labelled: "For the circumcised only", or would it be open to all who responded to the outgoing love of God shown in the Person of Jesus the Messiah?

Luke puts the issue clearly in Acts 15.1: "Some people ... from Judaea began to teach the brotherhood that those who were not circumcised in accordance with Mosaic practice could not be saved." A council took place in Jerusalem. There was no doubt that God had been at work in non-Jews to whom Paul and Barnabas had presented the good news. Why lay on their shoulders the unbearable yoke of circumcision? Peter saw and articulated the truth of the matter: "For our belief is that we are saved in the same way as they are: by the grace of the Lord Jesus." (Acts 15.11) The outcome of the deliberations of the council was that "they saw that [Paul] had been entrusted to take the gospel to the Gentiles as surely as Peter had been entrusted to take it to the Jews; for the same God who was at work in Peter's mission to the Jews was also in [Paul's] to the Gentiles" (Galatians 2.7–8). The good news was precisely the same for Jews and non-Jews. There was plenty of room for both stalwarts, Peter and Paul, to preach it. A hungry world, the vast majority of which was Gentile, awaited their message.

It may seem to some that a difference of opinion over a primitive rite, that of circumcision, is far removed from our concerns at the end of the second millennium. Superficially, it is, but the issue at the heart of the controversy could not be more relevant to present-day society. It has to do with the very nature of God, and the Church, and the Church's message to the world. The Jews had held that God had a very special place for them in his kingdom and in his economy – they were a favoured race. They were proud of this. The revelation to Paul and to Peter was that God has no preferences, no interest in labels and rites of entry to his kingdom. All are equal before him; for Christ there can be no barriers of race or colour ("there is no such thing as Jew and Greek"), no barriers of class (there is no such thing as "slave and freeman"), and no barriers of gender (there is no such thing as "male and female"), "for you are all one person in Christ Jesus"; "It is through faith that you are all sons of God in union with Christ Jesus" (Galatians 3.28, 26). We are back to the heading of this chapter, to the seminal phrase "in Christ".

In that phrase, which we have seen to be as much corporate as personal, is God's "No" to the curse of racial superiority, but how slow the Church has been in applying that uncomfortable doctrine to real-life situations. How slow we have been to stand behind those in South Africa who have sought to topple the idol of colour. How silent we have been in not making our sympathy with Mandela and Tutu clear from the start.

In that phrase "in Christ" is God's "No" to the barrier of class and privilege. Still, the right school tie, the "best" university, the background of wealth and privilege open doors to some which should be open to all.

In that phrase "in Christ" is God's "No" to the gender barrier, but how slow the Church has been to welcome the contribution of women to its task, and to understand that only when they are given free rein will the ministry of the Church be seen in its wholeness. The twentieth century has seen an awareness of these iniquities, and this is cause for thankfulness, but the Church still has much that calls for repentance. Too long have we refused to see the explosive power of those two words "in Christ", sheltering behind a pietistic use of them which deprives them of their disturbing dynamism.[10]

Paul, we have said, knew where to fight his battles for the fullness of the gospel. As a pastor, he knew that he must protect his flock from a different gospel which is no gospel at all (Galatians 1.6–9). It is a tribute to his faithfulness that, as a man "in Christ", he dared to spell out the down-to-earth meaning of those words. To ignore the dangers of false teachers or to succumb to their teachings would be to deny the universality of the gospel, to belittle the centrality of Christ, and to rob the Church of its virility.

Ephesians and Colossians

The letters to the Galatians and to the Romans expose the dangers of putting our trust in anything other than Christ alone. The letters to the Ephesians and to the Colossians expose another danger which attacked the early disciples of Jesus. Again, on first consideration, that could be seen as a danger which was urgent then but is irrelevant now. As a matter of fact, it is a danger which has recurred throughout history and is with us today. Paul, as a faithful pastor and as a "man in Christ", sought to deal with this, lest the members of the Body of Christ be led astray.

As Paul moved from city to city, from one gathering of Christians to another, he became aware of a philosophy which was gaining ground among thoughtful people and their often not-so-thoughtful followers. The seeds of what became a popular way of thinking, Gnosticism, were beginning to spring to life. The word *gnosis* simply means "knowledge". Some of those who subscribed to this way of thinking regarded knowledge as the key to unlock the mystery of God. For them, matter was evil, and therefore they denied the true humanity of Jesus. If we material beings were to reach the invisible God and have any kind of union with him, such union could not be achieved except through a series of emanations, a kind of ladder from humankind to God. So the argument ran.

Paul sometimes used the language of those who held these views to meet their challenge head on – writing, for example, of "invisible orders of thrones, sovereignties, authorities, and powers" (Colossians 1.16) – only to sweep them away as he insisted on the supremacy of Christ. There is no need for this ladder, he said. Christ himself is the answer; he is the one "through whom our release is secured and our sins are forgiven" (Colossians 1.14) – that in itself is a magnificent reality. We have been rescued and brought "into the kingdom of [God's] dear Son" (verse 13), he reminds us. Paul extended the range of his gospel through his cosmic view of Christ himself: "He is the image of the invisible God; his is the primacy over *all creation*." (verse 15, author's italics) Supreme over all, he holds all things together; without him creation would relapse into primitive chaos. This head of creation is also head of the Church, his Body. In him, in him alone, God's fullness dwells. He is the centre of the process of reconciliation. If you want gnosis, knowledge, you will find it in Christ himself (Colossians 2.3). That is the knowledge that counts: a matter of the heart and will as well as of the mind, *experiential* knowledge.

The secret of Christ's cosmic rule has been hidden for long ages, but now is disclosed. God's purpose for all mankind, for Jew and Gentile alike, has been made known, and the revelation centres in the crucified and risen Christ. "He it is whom we proclaim." (Colossians 1.28)[11]

What Paul, this "man in Christ", had to say about the uniqueness of Jesus Christ is of immediate relevance to us today. Two instances may be mentioned:

1 At the beginning of this century (to look back no further), the overseas missionary work of the Church was pursued with vigour and received the sacrificial service of some of its finest women and men. They left in their train a trail of light, in the sphere of evangelism, medicine and education. On the debit side of the account, we must confess to an element, sometimes strong, of Western insensitivity and "superiority". We presented certain facets of our Western culture as if they were of the essence of the Christian message, when in fact they were nothing of the sort. We rode roughshod over the cultures of the peoples to whom we took the gospel.

Now, it is to be hoped, our approach is more sensitive. We know far more about the religion of the world than did our forebears. Are we humble enough to learn from those who have drunk deeply at the wells of India's religions or entered into the insights of Buddhism? Were the devotees of the great world religions in total darkness before they were presented with the gospel of Christ? We can no longer engage in any approach which smacks of Western superiority.

The situation is made the more urgent by the invasion – I use the word in no pejorative sense – of large numbers of people from abroad into our cities and institutions. The problems thus created are legion. To take but one instance: what is to be done with the periods in school curricula hitherto given to Christian devotion and instruction? There are no easy answers. Some schools seek to meet the difficulty by using these periods for elementary lessons in comparative religions. That can be enlightening, but there are few people who are adequately trained to give such wide-ranging instruction. Another problem is the danger that, at the end of the day, the children in our schools will gain the impression that, as all religions are a groping after God, it matters little which, if any, they adopt.

Part of the "offence" of the Christian faith is the insistence that, in a given place in the Near East, at a given moment in history, came a Man, truly man, who was more than man. A revelation from God took place in his coming, in what he was and in what he did, which divided history into two: before Christ and after Christ. The word "unique", so often incorrectly used and qualified by another word, may rightly be used here. Christianity is unique because Christ is unique. "You have heard that our forefathers were told . . . but what I tell you is this." Never man spoke like this man. Christianity finds its focus in a revelation of divine activity, erupting into history – a saving event indeed. If this be the offence of the Christian faith, then we bear it, and we declare its message, but with utmost humility.

2 "He it is whom we proclaim." (Colossians 1.28) Christian "proclamation" takes many forms, at its best the form of a consistent *discipleship* of Jesus so patently clear that few

words are needed. Christian proclamation takes place when *drama* is so presented on the stage as to raise issues of ethical and moral importance and point in the direction where the message of the Christian faith may bring light to bear on the problems. There is a proclamation in the *arts*, when they make clear some facet of the Christian truth. But here I have in mind primarily the proclamation of the *pulpit*, proclamation such as Paul, that "man in Christ", engaged in when he preached in public and, in groups or with individuals, he "put his case to them; he spoke urgently of the kingdom of God" (Acts 28.23). "He it is whom we proclaim." I have heard sermons in which God and his Son are scarcely mentioned. Can such addresses be called sermons? Have they anything to declare? To whom do they point? In my book *A New Day for Preaching*, there is a chapter entitled: "Towards a Definition of Preaching". In it I quote from an entry in John Wesley's journal for 17 July 1739:

I rode to Bradford five miles from Bath. Some persons had pitched on a convenient place, on the top of a hill under which the town lies . . . There I offered Christ to about a thousand people, for wisdom, righteousness, sanctification and redemption.[12]

Old-fashioned language? Yes. But "I offered Christ" – let preachers look at their sermon-notes: "Him we proclaim"?

In the same chapter, I also quote Bernard Lord Manning's definition of preaching: "A manifestation of the Incarnate Word, from the Written Word, by the spoken word"[13] – a touchstone for true Christian preaching.

For Paul, proclamation included teaching and instruction in all the ways of wisdom. He sought *maturity* in the characters and witness of his friends. To this end he toiled "strenuously with all the energy and power of Christ at work in me" (Colossians 1.29). To be "a man in Christ" meant to be a man with pastoral care, building up a community whose members were equipped for mission, each "limb" of Christ's body fulfilling his or her function. Mission calls for a deep-rootedness in the faith combined with a great openness to the world; there can be no narrow pietism in one through whom the wind of Christ's Spirit blows.

Enough has been said in this chapter to make the point that we shall get close to the heart of Paul, "meet Paul", only if we enter into the phrase "in Christ". We shall get an angle on his character and religion when we consider him as theologian, evangelist or pastor; all these approaches will help us. But we shall penetrate to his heart when we enter into the meaning of those two monosyllables, "in Christ". The same is true if we are seeking to get to the heart of John's presentation of the Faith. "Dwell in me, as I in you. No branch can bear fruit by itself, but only if it remains united with the vine; . . . apart from me you can do nothing." (John 15.1ff.) Here the two great New Testament figures, Paul and John, join hands – "in Christ", "in the vine" – in all the intimacy of personal experience, in all the power of membership of Christ's Body.

We must go further. We dare to say that in those two words, "in Christ", *we get nearest to the heart of God*. The God who is "King of kings and Lord of lords, who alone possesses immortality, dwelling in unapproachable light, whom no one has ever seen or can ever see" (1 Timothy 6.15–16) has made himself known in Christ, his "image, his *icon*, the human face of the infinite, 'the side of God turned toward us'".[14]

Perhaps we had best leave the last word to the poets, for they can sometimes say what we poor stammerers find hard to verbalise. George Herbert, seventeenth-century poet and divine, puts it in his own quaint way in his poem 'Aaron':

> Christ is my only head,
> My alone only heart and breast,
> My only music, striking me ev'n dead;

That to the old man I may rest,
And be in Him new drest.[15]

F. W. H. Myers (1843–1901) puts it more robustly than the gentle George Herbert. He strikes a strong autobiographical note as, in his poem 'St Paul', he pays tribute to his Master and Paul's:

Who that one moment has at least descried him,
Dimly and faintly, hidden and afar,
Does not despise all excellence beside him,
Pleasures and powers that are not and that are?

This hath he done and shall we not adore him?
This shall he do and can we still despair?
Come let us quickly fling ourselves before him,
Cast at his feet the burthen of our care.

Flash from our eyes the glow of our thanksgiving,
Glad and regretful, confident and calm,
Then thro' all life and what is after living
Thrill to the tireless music of a psalm.

Yea, thro' life, death, thro' sorrow and thro' sinning,
He shall suffice me, for he hath sufficed.
Christ is the end, for Christ is the beginning,
Christ the beginning, for the end is Christ.[16]

Prayers

O God,
who in the work of creation
commanded the light to shine out of darkness:
we pray that the light of the glorious gospel of Christ
may shine into the hearts of all your people,
dispelling the darkness of ignorance and unbelief
and revealing to them the knowledge of your glory
in the face of Christ Jesus our Lord.[17]

O Jesus, Master Carpenter of Nazareth,
who on the cross through wood and nails hast
    wrought man's full salvation:
wield well thy tools in this thy workshop,
that we who come to thee rough-hewn
may be fashioned to a truer beauty by thy hand,
who with the Father and the Holy Spirit
livest one God, world without end.[18]

Grant
complete trust in thee,
immediate reference to thee,
utter dependence on thee,
always, O blessed Lord.[19]

Christ be with me,
Christ within me,
Christ behind me,
Christ before me,
Christ to seek me,
Christ to win me,
Christ to comfort and restore me.[20]

Questions

1 Jesus was a man of the country, Paul a man of the city. How did this difference affect their respective presentations of the truth?

2 Did Paul misinterpret the message of Jesus? Or did he expound its essentials?

3 Paul was a missionary strategist. Judging from your reading of Acts and of the Pauline letters, what were the main thrusts of that strategy?

4 Race, class, gender – these may be said to have been the main divisive elements in first-century society. They remain much the same in our day. What had/has Paul to say about these matters?

5 Paul and Luke were great friends. It was a relationship fruitful to them both. In what ways?

6 Paul describes himself as a slave of Jesus Christ, as an apostle, and (by implication) as a son of the Father-God. In what ways do these words reveal the character of the man?

7 "This one thing I do" (Philippians 3.13, AV). Restrictive, or liberating?

8 What difference has the reading of this book made to you in your understanding of (a) Paul himself, and (b) his message?

9 When you meet Paul in the life to come, what will you most thank him for? What question will you most urgently put to him?

—— Notes ——

All biblical quotations are from *The Revised English Bible*, Oxford University Press and Cambridge University Press, 1989, unless otherwise indicated.
D. C. = written by the author.

CHAPTER 1

1. Helmut Thielicke, *Notes from a Wayfarer* (James Clarke, 1995), p. 280.
2. The question of authenticity or inauthenticity of the other [letters] can be left out of account here; in any case, no consensus can be reached over a solution, even with the use of the same philological and historical criteria. I have therefore cited relevant verses from "disputed" writings for investigating prayer in Paul. For they are so manifestly in line with the passages to be used from the undisputed letters that we may assume that some disciples of Paul faithfully carried on the master's practice and views of prayer. Whether they come from Paul or his disciples, the disputed letters at any rate help to fill out the picture. (Oscar Cullman, *Prayer in the New Testament* (SCM Press, 1995), p. 69.)
   I am in agreement with that approach.
3. E. Hennecke, *New Testament Apocrypha* (*Study Edition*), vol. 2 (SCM Press, 1974), p. 354.
4. Collect for the Conversion of St Paul, *The Alternative Service Book 1980*.
5. D. C.
6. D. C.

CHAPTER 2

1. Bishop Stephen Neill, *God's Apprentice* (Hodder & Stoughton, 1991).

109

2. From the Latin *cui servire est regnare*, "whom to serve is to reign", Second Collect of Morning Prayer, *Book of Common Prayer 1662*.
3. Basil Hume, *Searching for God* (Hodder, 1977).
4. Olive Wyon, quoted by Janet Crawford in *Ecumenical Pilgrims: Profiles of Pioneers in Christian Reconciliation* (W.C.C., 1995), p. 241.
5. In his *Footfalls in Memory: Reflections from Solitude* (Hodder & Stoughton, 1995, pp. 95–96) Terry Waite quotes from Carlo Carretto's *Letters from the Desert*:

   > When I first came to the Sahara I was afraid of the night. For some, night means more work, for others dissipation, for still others insomnia, boredom.
   >
   > For me now it's quite different. Night is first of all rest, real rest. At sunset a great serenity sets in, as though nature were obeying a sudden sign from God. The wind which has howled all day ceases, the heat dies down, the atmosphere becomes clear and limpid, and great peace spreads everywhere, as though man and the elements wanted to refresh themselves after the great battle with the day and its sun . . . Time passes undisturbed. No obligations harass you, no noise disturbs you, no worry awaits you; time is all yours. So you satiate yourself with prayer and silence, while the stars light up in the sky . . .

6. Source unknown.
7. D. C.
8. D. C.

CHAPTER 3

1. *The Mystery of Salvation: The Story of God's Gift, A Report by the Doctrine Commission of the General Synod of the Church of England* (Church House Publishing, 1995), p. 38.
2. Martin Israel, *Dark Victory: Through Depression to Hope* (Mowbray, 1995), pp. 141–2.
3. Elizabeth Roberts and Ann Shukman (eds), *Christianity for the Twenty-First Century: The Life and Work of Alexander Men* (SCM Press, 1996), p. 190.
4. If Paul's use of the phrase "the kingdom of God" is rare compared with the frequency of its occurrence in the teaching of Jesus – and that is the case – it need not surprise us. Paul wrote to a world dominated by a Roman emperor. Constantly to refer to another king (Jesus) would have been to wave a red rag in the face of a bull. Had not Jesus told his disciples to be "wise as serpents" (Matthew 10:16)?
5. *A New Day for Preaching* (SPCK, 1996), pp. 113ff.

6. Henry Chadwick (ed), *Saint Augustine, Bishop of Hippo – Confessions* (Oxford University Press, 1991), p. ix.
7. —, p. 40.
8. —, p. 59.
9. —, pp. 131–2
10. Roland Bainton, *Here I Stand* (Lion, 1978), pp. 60, 65.
11. —, p. 65.
12. D. C.
13. D. C. (adapted from *The Alternative Service Book 1980*, p. 462).

CHAPTER 4

1. *Saint Augustine, Bishop of Hippo – Confessions* (see Chapter 3, note 6, above) p. 130.
2. Helmut Thielicke, German theologian and preacher, at the end of his autobiography, looked back over his life, a considerable part of which "was filled with my quest for truth". He wrote:

   My profession involved the interpretation of ancient texts, which I sought to penetrate until I rediscovered in them my own questions about life and those of my generation. In this mirror I saw these questions – *sub specie aeternitatis*, so to speak – light up anew: "In your light we see the light". To many contemporaries it seemed and still seems grotesque to consult an ancient book, that is, the Bible, on where we have come from and where we are going, and with its help to fathom the purpose for which we have been created. Can we not send our probes into space? Are we not constantly on the hunt for the novel, for "innovations", if I may employ a magic word from the computer world? Is it thus not backward to take this other route when dealing with the fundamental truths of our lives? Is it not retrogressive to grope one's way towards the ancient places where God left his tracks, the places which he deemed worthy of his presence, and where he uttered his command "Let there be" in ever new variations?

   In my long life I have seen so many truths claiming to be the "last word" come and go like nine-day wonders! How comical the gods of the day seem just a few hours later, how absurd they look from behind! . . . I, on the other hand, felt myself through this ancient book to be already facing the future, namely that period in the future that would make clear the futility of the gods of the day and testify to the strength of this one God. (*Notes from a Wayfarer* (James Clarke, 1995), pp. 416–17)

Another German theologian and preacher, Gerd Theissen, gives five sample sermons which show how passages of ancient Scripture relate to modern life and its problems (*The Sign Language of Faith* (SCM, 1995), pp. 130ff.).
3. See also Chapter 6.
4. There is much to be said for the view that verse 25b has got out of place and should be put at the end of verse 23. It is a summary of the main argument of Romans, Chapter 7. The triumphant thanksgiving of verse 25a then serves as an introduction to Romans 8 – "thanks be to him through Jesus Christ our Lord . . . no condemnation . . . freedom from the law of sin and death".
5. C. H. Dodd, *The Epistle to the Romans* (Hodder & Stoughton, 1932), p. 109.
6. Based on Ephesians 3: 14–19.
7. D. C.
8. D. C.
9. D. C.
10. D. C.

CHAPTER 5

1. *Ecumenical Pilgrims* (see Chapter 2, note 4, above), p. 227.
2. In the following pages, I have drawn on pp. 126ff. of my book, *The Prayers of the New Testament* (Hodder & Stoughton, 1967).
3. J. S. Whale, *Christian Doctrine*, (CUP, 1942), p. 126.
4. Source unknown.
5. Pope John XXIII, *Diary of a Soul* (Geoffrey Chapman, 1965).

CHAPTER 6

1. It was said of Dorothy Day, that colourful pioneer of Christian reconciliation, that "she found that whenever she went walking, she was praying and the prayers were entirely of joy and gratitude" (*Ecumenical Pilgrims*, p. 78 – see Chapter 2, note 4, above).
2. In this paragraph on Ashkenazy, I have drawn on pp. 21–2 of my book *A New Day for Preaching* (SPCK, 1996).
3. *Christianity for the Twenty-First Century: The Life and Work of Alexander Men* (see Chapter 3, note 3, above).
4.–6. ——, pp. 187–9.
7. *A Version of the Daily Office SSF* (Mowbray, 1994), p. 230.
8. *Ecumenical Pilgrims*, p. 179 (see Chapter 2, note 4, above).

9. Franklin C. Fry in *Ecumenical Pilgrims*, pp. 97–8 (see Chapter 2, note 4, above).
10. On the position of women in the world of Paul's day, and on his attitude to them, I have written more fully in *Paul: Portrait of a Revolutionary* (Hodder & Stoughton, 1984), pp. 160–66.
11. Those who wish to pursue this further will find a study of 1 Corinthians 1 helpful.
12. *A New Day for Preaching* (SPCK, 1996), pp. 37ff.
13. ——, p. 39.
14. M. J. Borg, *Meeting Jesus again for the First Time*, p. 137 (publisher unknown).
15. *The Works of George Herbert* (Wordsworth Poetry Library, 1994), p. 162.
16. Source unknown.
17. *Celebrating Common Prayer*, p. 176 (see note 7, above).
18. Source unknown.
19. George Appleton, *Jerusalem Prayers for the World Today* (SPCK, 1974).
20. "St Patrick's Breastplate" *Hymns Ancient and Modern* (revised 1950), p. 162.

The Society for Promoting Christian Knowledge (SPCK) has as
its purpose three main tasks:

- **Communicating the Christian faith in its rich diversity**

- **Helping people to understand the Christian faith
  and to develop their personal faith**

- **Equipping Christians for mission and ministry**

SPCK Worldwide serves the Church through Christian
literature and communication projects in over 100 countries.
Special schemes also provide books for those training for
ministry in many parts of the developing world. SPCK
Worldwide's ministry involves Churches of many traditions.
This worldwide service depends upon the generosity of others
and all gifts are spent wholly on ministry programmes,
without deductions.

SPCK Bookshops support the life of the Christian community
by making available a full range of Christian literature and other
resources, and by providing support to bookstalls and book agents
throughout the UK. SPCK Bookshops' mail order department meets
the needs of overseas customers and those unable to have access to
local bookshops.

SPCK Publishing produces Christian books and resources,
covering a wide range of inspirational, pastoral, practical and
academic subjects. Authors are drawn from many different Christian
traditions, and publications aim to meet the needs of a wide variety of
readers in the UK and throughout the world.

The Society does not necessarily endorse the individual views con-
tained in its publications, but hopes they stimulate readers to think
about and further develop their Christian faith.

For further information about the Society, please write to:
SPCK, Holy Trinity Church, Marylebone Road,
London NW1 4DU, United Kingdom.
Telephone: 0171 387 5282